CHARLES DICKENS

CHARLES DICKENS

from the portrait of 1839 by Daniel Maclise (1806-1870) by courtesy of the National Portrait Gallery, London

CHARLES DICKENS

ROD MENGHAM

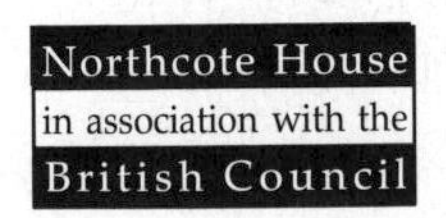

First published in 2001 by Northcote House Publishers Ltd, Horndon, Tavistock, Devon, PL19 9NQ, United Kingdom.
Tel: +44 (01822) 810066 Fax: +44 (01822) 810034.

British Library Cataloguing-in-Publication Data
A catalogue record for this book is available from the British Library

ISBN 0-7463-0801-9

Typeset by PDQ Typesetting, Newcastle-under-Lyme
Printed and bound in the United Kingdom

Contents

Biographical Outline vii
Abbreviations ix
Introduction 1

1 Streetwise 2
2 The Image of the Child 21
3 Authority and Rebellion 37
4 First Person 52
5 Taking the Roof Off 72
6 The Stupendous Power of Money 84
7 Divided Selves 102
8 Concluding 120

Notes 127
Select Bibliography 128
Index 133

Biographical Outline

1812	Born, 7 February, Landport, Portsmouth. Second child and eldest son of John Dickens, a clerk in the Navy Pay Office, and Elizabeth Dickens (née Barrow).
1814	John Dickens transferred to Somerset House; family moves to London.
1817	Family moves to Chatham. Charles begins school.
1822	Family moves back to London, where Charles's schooling is not resumed.
1824	John Dickens imprisoned for debt in the Marshalsea. The family moves into the prison, except for Charles, who lodges separately and is sent to work at Warrens's Blacking. After five months, he resumes schooling at Wellington House Academy.
1827	Employed as office boy at Ellis and Blackmore, attorneys of Gray's Inn. Learns shorthand.
1828	Freelance shorthand reporter in Doctors' Commons.
1831	Falls in love with Maria Beadnell.
1832	Works as shorthand reporter for the *Mirror of Parliament*, transcribing proceedings, and for the *True Sun*.
1833	Relationship with Maria Beadnell ends. First publication, 'A Dinner at Poplar Walk', in the *Monthly Magazine*.
1834	Parliamentary reporter for the *Morning Chronicle*.
1835	Contributes sketches to *Evening Chronicle*, edited by George Hogarth. Engaged to Catherine Hogarth in April.
1836	Marries Catherine. Publication of *Sketches by Boz*. Starts work on *The Pickwick Papers* and resigns from the *Morning Chronicle*.
1837	Finishes *The Pickwick Papers*. Editor of *Bentley's Miscellany*. Sister-in-law Mary Hogarth dies. Birth of first child, Charles.

1838	*Oliver Twist.*
1839	*Nicholas Nickleby.*
1841	*The Old Curiosity Shop; Barnaby Rudge.*
1842	Travels in United States. *American Notes for General Circulation.*
1843	*A Christmas Carol.*
1844	Residing in Genoa. Changes publisher, from Chapman and Hall to Bradbury and Evans. *Martin Chuzzlewit; The Chimes.*
1845	Returns from Italy. *The Cricket on the Hearth.*
1846	*Pictures from Italy.* Edits *Daily News.*
1847	Opens Urania Cottage, a refuge for fallen women in Shepherd's Bush.
1848	*Dombey and Son.*
1850	*David Copperfield.* Begins editing *Household Words.*
1851	Joseph Paxton shows Dickens the Crystal Palace. Father dies.
1853	*Bleak House.* Travels in France, Italy, and Switzerland with Wilkie Collins.
1854	*Hard Times.*
1855	Residing in Paris.
1856	Buys Gad's Hill Place, near Rochester.
1857	*Little Dorrit.* Meets the actress Ellen Ternan.
1858	Separates from his wife. Makes a public statement about his 'domestic trouble' in *Household Words.* First public reading for profit, 29 April.
1859	*A Tale of Two Cities.* Begins editing *All the Year Round.*
1861	*Great Expectations.*
1863	Mother dies.
1865	*Our Mutual Friend.* 'Dr Marigold's Prescriptions'. Dickens and Ellen Ternan involved in railway accident at Staplehurst.
1867	Reading tour of America.
1868	Farewell reading tour. Begins *The Mystery of Edwin Drood.*
1870	Final Farewell Reading in London. Suffers a stroke and dies 9 June

Abbreviations

AFW — 'An Appeal to Fallen Women', in *The Letters of Charles Dickens*, v. *1847–1849*, ed. Graham Storey and K. J. Fielding (Oxford: Clarendon Press, 1981), appendix D

AN — *American Notes for General Circulation*, ed. Arnold Goldman and John Whitley (Harmondsworth: Penguin Books, 1972)

BH — *Bleak House*, ed. Nicola Bradbury (Harmondsworth: Penguin Books, 1997)

BR — *Barnaby Rudge*, ed. Gordon Spence (Harmondsworth: Penguin Books, 1997)

DC — *David Copperfield*, ed. Jeremy Tambling (Harmondsworth: Penguin Books, 1996)

DS — *Dombey and Son*, ed. Peter Fairclough, with an Introduction by Raymond Williams (Harmondsworth: Penguin Books, 1985)

GE — *Great Expectations*, ed. Angus Calder (Harmondsworth: Penguin Books, 1965)

HT — *Hard Times*, ed. Kate Flint (Harmondsworth: Penguin Books, 1995)

L. — *The Letters of Charles Dickens*, iv. *1844–1846*, ed. Kathleen Tillotson (Oxford: Clarendon Press, 1977); v. *1847–1849*, ed. Graham Storey and K. J. Fielding (Oxford: Clarendon Press, 1981); ix. *1859–61*, ed. Graham Storey (Oxford: Clarendon Press, 1997)

LD — *Little Dorrit*, ed. John Holloway (Harmondsworth: Penguin Books, 1996)

MC — *Martin Chuzzlewit*, ed. Patricia Ingham (Harmondsworth: Penguin Books, 1999)

MED — *The Mystery of Edwin Drood*, ed. Arthur J. Cox, with an Introduction by Angus Wilson (Harmondsworth: Penguin Books, 1985)

NN	*Nicholas Nickleby*, ed. Mark Ford (Harmondsworth: Penguin Books, 1999)
OCS	*The Old Curiosity Shop*, ed. Angus Easson, with an Introduction by Malcolm Andrews (Harmondsworth: Penguin Books, 1972)
OMF	*Our Mutual Friend*, ed. Adrian Poole (Harmondsworth: Penguin Books, 1999)
OT	*Oliver* Twist, ed. Angus Wilson (Harmondsworth: Penguin Books, 1966)
PP	*The Pickwick Papers*, ed. Mark Wormald (Harmondsworth: Penguin Books, 1999)
S.	*The Speeches of Charles Dickens*, ed. K. J. Fielding (Hemel Hempstead: Harvester, 1988)
SB	*Sketches by Boz, and Other Early Papers, 1833–39*, ed. Michael Slater (London: Dent, 1994)
SJ	*Selected Journalism 1850-1870*, ed. David Pascoe (Harmondsworth: Penguin Books, 1997)
SN	*Sikes and Nancy and Other Public Readings*, ed. Philip Collins (Oxford: Oxford University Press, 1983)
TTC	*A Tale of Two Cities*, ed. George Woodcock (Harmondsworth: Penguin Books, 1988)

Introduction

This study of Dickens touches on all the major fiction. It is organized thematically, but the order in which the several themes are examined reflects the progress of Dickens's career. For those readers who prefer to be given a sense of the writer's development, there is this rough chronological sequence; otherwise, the various chapters could be regarded as preliminary discussions of concerns and compulsions that recur at every stage, and in every aspect, of Dickens's work.

It is of course impossible in this very short book to do justice to so many crowded and lengthy novels. Rather than write briefly about each one, I have chosen to give relatively comprehensive readings of a few, in order to demonstrate in some detail the systematic complexity of Dickens's writing. Those texts that have received the more thoroughgoing treatment fall, either wholly or in part, into the category of first-person narratives.

It is through the use of the first person in novels, letters, and travel writings that Dickens reveals a good deal not only about his own identity, but also about the construction of Victorian subjectivity in general. The overriding focus of the analyses in this book is a literary one, although it also includes a series of reflections on aspects of Victorian society and culture: prisons, schools, money, poverty, fallen women, orphans, detectives, crowds, the Great Exhibition; Dickens is forever tracing the connections between these different facets of life in Victorian Britain. The manner in which he makes these connections is both unique and symptomatic – the product of an individual psychology and the basis of a cultural poetics.

1

Streetwise

SKETCHES BY BOZ, THE PICKWICK PAPERS

From the very start, a major element in Dickens's career as a writer was his recognition of the strangeness of life in the nineteenth-century city. *Sketches by Boz* (1833–6) represents an early attempt to investigate and grasp the nature of an environment that had totally revolutionized the lives of its inhabitants within the space of a few decades. During Dickens's youth and early adulthood, increasingly large numbers of British people were gravitating towards an urban lifestyle; by 1851, when a census was taken, a clear majority lived in cities and large towns. It had taken only one or two generations for most British people to exchange the pace of existence in the smaller-scale communities of the rural areas for the experience of living with, or in, the crowd. The change of scale created problems of intelligibility and orientation, obstructions to a sense of belonging, difficulties in the way of what the critic Raymond Williams has referred to as 'knowability'.

In the smaller towns and villages of pre-industrial England, a walk down the high street would have involved encounters with other people many of whom would be familiar to the individual observer, but in the rapidly expanding centres of population in Victorian England perhaps the vast majority of those passing in the street would be, and would remain, unknown. In the earlier situation, the observer would be able to match the outward appearance of many passers-by with some knowledge of their character and relations: the experience of the street would involve frequent brushes with individuals with a definite past. But in the teeming cities of the industrial era, there would be a crowd of faces without names or histories, a variety of surfaces without depth.

Dickens testifies to the novelty and strangeness of this shift in social perceptions in his earliest published writings, composed in the early to mid-1830s. He remarks on the bizarre combination of anonymity with mere visual familiarity in his descriptions of waves of middle-aged men walking to work through the streets of London. These are figures who 'plod steadily along, apparently with no object in view but the counting-house; knowing by sight almost everybody they meet or overtake, for they have seen them every morning (Sundays excepted) during the last twenty years, but speaking to no one'(*SB* 53). And once anonymity has become the norm it alters the tone of relations even between those who do recognize each other:

> If they do happen to overtake a personal acquaintance, they just exchange a hurried salutation, and keep walking on, either by his side or in front of him, as his rate of walking may chance to be. As to stopping to shake hands, or to take the friend's arm, they seem to think that as it is not included in their salary, they have no right to do it. (*SB* 53–4)

Dickens is clearly emphasizing here the unnaturalness of the crowd's behaviour, even while he is ready to extract amusement from it. But a much more anxious reaction to the barrier of anonymity is given in a classic statement of the mid-nineteenth century cityscape in Edgar Allen Poe's short story, 'The Man of the Crowd', published for the first time just a few years later in 1840, in *Burton's Gentleman's Magazine*. Poe's narrator observes the crowd on a London street and categorizes its members according to visual clues; this sorting operation proceeds quite mechanically until he is suddenly overwhelmed with curiosity over the features of a face that 'does not permit itself to be read'. Fascinated by the enigmatic nature of this face, the narrator goes off in pursuit of its significance, acting like a private detective on the tail of a suspect, keeping his man in view while remaining out of sight himself. After an exhausting and completely aimless tramp through various districts of London during one evening and night and the whole of the next day, the narrator is forced to conclude that the 'man of the crowd' is a fundamental mystery:

> 'This old man,' I said at length, 'is the type and the genius of deep crime. He refuses to be alone. *He is the man of the crowd.* It will be in vain to follow; for I shall learn no more of him, nor of his deeds. The

> worst heart of the world is a grosser book than the "Hortulus Animae", and perhaps it is but one of the great mercies of God that *es lasst sich nicht lesen* [it does not permit itself to be read].[1]

The narrator's decision to resign from the pursuit of meaning brings relief and is almost a form of blessed release; anonymity is threatening, unreadability induces feelings of dread and of deep, even paranoid, suspicion. The anxiety of Poe's narrator helps to account for the popularity of phrenology during the 1830s and 1840s; this pseudo-scientific method of discovering character through the interpretation of cranial bumps responds to a widely felt need to restore connections between surfaces and depths, between physical appearance and psychological reality. Of course, the spuriousness of phrenology, once recognized, has the opposite effect of that intended; far from acting as a guarantee of meaning, it permits misrecognition, a conflict of interpretations, wild analysis. It stems from the realization that there is no automatic correspondence between interior and exterior, yet its fraudulence means that, far from solving the problem, it only exacerbates it.

Dickens satirizes the mania for phrenological interpretation in his fantasy on door knockers in the seventh chapter of *Sketches by Boz*:

> Some phrenologists affirm, that the agitation of a man's brain by different passions, produces corresponding developments in the form of his skull. Do not let us be understood as pushing our theory to the full length of asserting, that any alteration in a man's disposition would produce a visible effect on the feature of his knocker. Our position merely is, that in such a case, the magnetism which must exist between a man and his knocker, would induce the man to remove, and seek some knocker more congenial to his altered feelings. (*SB* 43)

The lightness of touch here is typical of *Sketches by Boz*. It is a text that broaches many of the topics to be developed in Dickens's later work, but with less of the unease that they will go on to explore. There is a marked difference in tone between Poe and Boz; while Poe's narrator is haunted and depressed, Dickens's is irrepressible, and his incremental absurdities provide the model for a whole career in which the imagination overcompensates giddily for unreadability. When faced by the barrier of anonymity, of unknowability, figured in this passage as quite precisely a threshold between public and private, Dickens neither retreats from, nor effaces, the crisis of interpretation but regards it as a stimulus to the powers of an imagination forever outdoing itself in the rush to find new meanings to read into whatever material is offering resistance. A celebrated instance is provided in *Sketches by Boz* by the 'Scene' entitled 'Meditations in Monmouth Street', where the narrator fancifully reconstructs a whole series of life histories, from the evidence alone of a few sets of old clothes, on the principle that 'There was the whole man's life written as legibly on those clothes, as if we had his autobiography engrossed on parchment before us' (*SB* 78).

But, however fanciful, Dickens's narratorial acrobatics do not prevent him from registering the profound psychological unease generated by the predominance of the unknowable. At every stage of his career, there is constant evidence of a desperate urge to translate the unknowable into the knowable by penetrating beyond the appearance of things. And Dickens is aware of the extent to which an individual compulsion to master things by seeing through them was being reflected in the 1820s and 1830s in the setting-up and the operation of a whole series of shared projects fuelled by the desire to establish new ways of knowing the world on a scientific basis. Organizations such as the Society for the Diffusion of Useful Knowledge and the British Association for the Advancement of Science are precisely what gave him the idea for his fictional creations the Mudfog Association and the Pickwick Club. Much of the writing in *The Pickwick Papers* (1836–7) is motivated by a concern to establish criteria for the practices of reading and knowing – criteria that emerge in the wake of Dickens's satirizing of misreadings and of an overreaching spirit of enquiry. The paradox here is that Dickens's own virtuosity is nowhere more apparent than in his systematic undermining of the Pickwickians' weakness for over-ingenious interpretation. A brilliant example of this is provided by the episode in which Mr Pickwick makes his 'immortal discovery, which has been the pride and boast of his friends, and the envy of every antiquarian in this or any other country' (*PP* 147). The discovery is of an old stone, set in the roadway in the village of Cobham, which is uprooted at Mr Pickwick's request by a labourer living nearby who is prepared to affirm that 'It was here long afore I war born, or any on us' (*PP* 147). Mr Pickwick's ecstasy at this discovery knows even fewer bounds than usual, especially after the stone has been cleaned, with the result that a 'fragment of an inscription was clearly to be deciphered':

+
B I L S T
U M
P S H I
S.M.
A R K

The fragmentary inscription drives Mr Pickwick on to his greatest achievement: the composition of a pamphlet, ninety-six pages long, which contains no less than twenty-seven different readings of the inscription. Other recorded reactions apart from Mr Pickwick's include those of 'three old gentlemen [who] cut off their eldest sons with a shilling a-piece for presuming to doubt the antiquity of the fragment' and of 'one enthusiastic individual [who] cut himself off prematurely, in despair at being unable to fathom its meaning' (*PP* 157). Once the illegibility of the fragment has been confirmed by the number of different meanings attributable to it, the apparatus of commentary and interpretation becomes self-perpetuating:

> seventeen learned societies, native and foreign, being roused, several fresh pamphlets appeared; the foreign learned societies corresponded with the native learned societies; the native learned societies translated the pamphlets of the foreign learned societies into English; the foreign learned societies translated the pamphlets of the native learned societies into all sorts of languages; and thus commenced that celebrated scientific discussion so well known to all men, as the Pickwick controversy. (*PP* 158)

What Mr Pickwick starts up, what is generated by his example, is a process of multiplication, or proliferation, although the origin of this proliferation is quite precisely the mark of an irreducible individuality – because what is discovered by the egregious Mr Blotton, who interviews the labourer in question, is that the simple, linear reading of the inscription is best: 'BILL STUMPS, HIS MARK'. The labourer who had vouched for the antiquity of the stone to Mr Pickwick had not vouched for the antiquity of the inscription, which he had carved himself.

We are not given any of Mr Pickwick's twenty-seven different readings of the inscription, but what we do learn is that his apprehension of brute reality is ingenuous, naïve, credulous, risible in some respects, but that it also represents a creative energy, a desire to promote understanding, to complete what is fragmentary, to repair what is broken, to restore what is lost. The members of the Pickwick Club express their admiration of him with a gift of gold spectacles, and the gift itself conveys the same tension of qualities: Mr Pickwick needs glasses because he cannot see what is staring him in the face, but at the same time this is something of a virtue – a gilt-edged defect, so to speak – when it elevates the commonplace, romanticizes the sterile, harmonizes the discordant. Mr Pickwick lives in a world of societies: small communities of savants who collaborate in each other's researches and duplicate each other's views. Mr Blotton introduces a sour note of solitary, individualistic dissent. Moreover, he disrupts the aura of respectability that clings to the very idea of being a member of a learned society. The cast of Blotton's mind is 'vulgar' and 'degrading', and the reading he favours is a crude one: a triumph of near-illiteracy, irredeemably proletarian. Disruption, dissent, and a brand of selfish individualism, then, are connected with an attack against that gentility of which Pickwick is such an extraordinary representative; if in so many other ways he is a clear descendant of the heroes of eighteenth-century picaresque novels, he is at least original in the refinement and harmlessness of his appetites. It has been noted how unmasculine Pickwick is, in conventional terms; his virtues are the traditionally feminine ones of giving, caring, healing.

Blotton stands for roughness and boorishness (his name has associations with ugliness and clumsiness) but he also operates by a reality principle that the narrator cannot fault. Throughout the episode, the narrator borrows the tones and attitudes of a supporter of Pickwick, so that when he mimics the condemnation of Blotton – whose interpretation is called 'ridiculous' – the very excessiveness of the condemnation is a guarantee that the reader will be amused at Pickwick's expense. It is easy to see how the whole episode of the discovery of the stone might be regarded as a model for the divided consciousness of the writer faced with serial publication and the attendant problems of artistic form: on the one hand, he feels the need, and the ambition, to force into a shape what is broken and discontinuous; on the other hand, he can see the sense in, and indeed feels braced by, having to satisfy the more popular and lowbrow demand for self-contained, individual units of narrative. But this division obscures the importance of a third element in the passage. Blotton and Pickwick are obviously in opposition to each other, but they are in some ways even more in opposition, both of them, to something else: the weight of public opinion, the stampede of orthodoxy that results, among other things, in three old gentlemen cutting off their eldest sons with a shilling a-piece for presuming to doubt the antiquity of the fragment – and one enthusiastic individual cutting himself off prematurely, in despair at being unable to fathom its meaning. Of course, when one comes at these pathetic cases in their narrative context, they afford nothing but laughing matter, but when one takes them out of context, one does not have to take them very far to see that these social casualties, the subjects of personal catastrophe, are nothing other than protagonists in the world of the interpolated stories – that other strand in *The Pickwick Papers* that is less easy to remember: because it is devoid of humour, consists of relentlessly bleak accounts of victimizations, of unnatural conflicts between parents and children and between husbands and wives; a world disfigured by the absence of conciliation, pity, mercy, forgiveness; a world, above all, of divisions and isolations that would completely alienate the diplomatic and affable Pickwick. The three old gentlemen and the enthusiastic individual are obliquely, but emphatically, connected with the violence of this world through the black humour of the wordplay that links the disinheriting – one kind of 'cutting off' – with the much more literal cutting that ends the despair of the baffled individual. These are spectacular penalties to pay for either deliberate nonconformism or the inability to conform. Blotton's fate is much less exciting; however, he is persecuted with fervour, and the cost of his gesture of independence is to be expelled into an intellectual and social solitary confinement.

It is appropriate that the artistic form of the interpolated tales is stiflingly conventional. They are almost uniformly sombre in theme and ghastly in tone, and move towards wholly foreseeable conclusions. The story-telling technique is stolid and undeviating, in obvious contrast to the brilliant, swerving unpredictability of the comic frame. What I am suggesting is that the hidden lines of tension between these three forces, or principles, represented in this instance by Pickwick, Blotton, and a cruel orthodoxy, are latent throughout the book, and that the text at any point functions to repeat this triangulation.

The book actually starts with a ray of light, which is the purest expression of the Pickwick principle. Pickwick launches himself out of bed on the morning of the first journey in a repetition of this originary moment, which sheds light on the formation of the Pickwick Club, breathes life and warmth into the characters, generating them, as it were, out of nothing, because their past existences are left in complete obscurity: 'Mr Samuel Pickwick burst like another sun from his slumbers, threw open his chamber window, and looked out upon the world beneath' (*PP* 20). The mode is burlesque, but, despite the humorous aggrandizement, Pickwick goes on to display all the qualities inherent in the comparison of comforting, nurturing, and supporting all those who come within the sphere of his influence, all those for whom Pickwick is the centre of a self-contained world. His offices can be fundamentally life-giving, since much of the setting to rights in the book takes the form of physical relief, the provision of food and drink with which Mr Pickwick salves the wounded sensibilities of his followers. His instinctive benevolence is conveyed by the sunlike 'beaming' of his countenance at every available opportunity. On the other hand, when his mastery of a situation is in doubt (when he is drunk, for example), his fluctuating capacity for brilliance is compared to the vicissitudes of a gas lamp.

As the centre of his club, and of acquaintances of members of the club, Pickwick represents an apex of generosity, of purity of motive, and of strenuous goodwill. He starts with an unbounded confidence in the power of kindness, the ubiquity of honesty, and the lasting efficacy of reconciliations. But unfortunately for the Pickwickians, the establishment of their club coincides with a decision to trespass beyond the limits of their self-contained world. They are to be a 'corresponding society' whose members will have to travel to gain knowledge. This would have come as no surprise to the readers of eighteenth-century novels, for whom travelling was coextensive with moral education; but here it is aligned with learning of a very dilettantish sort, albeit pursued in the belief that, if it is properly reported, it will somehow be of general benefit to mankind. What the Pickwickians rapidly discover is that the world has nothing to teach them of which they can make any sense, because the influence of Mr Pickwick does not reach beyond his friends, and his philanthropic ideals are either ignored or derided in the world outside. Instead of the stability and security of the heliocentric Pickwickian world, they encounter confusion, trickery, and violence: institutionalized indifference and legalized injustice. To begin with, the consequences are not serious, and the childish ineptness of the Pickwickians merely offers scope for the reader's condescending mirth – it is simply that the practicalities of life are beyond them; they get caught between two advancing regiments in chapter four; they are powerless to control two refractory horses in chapter five. There soon comes a point, however, when the incomprehension of the Pickwickians provides the narrator with a means of ventilating his social criticisms. Already in chapter two, the presuppositions of Pickwick himself convert his account of the behaviour of a drunken soldier into a series of unintended sarcasms:

> The barmaid had positively refused to draw him any more liquor; in return for which he had (merely in playfulness) drawn his bayonet, and wounded the girl in the shoulder. And yet this fine fellow was the very first to go down to the house next morning, and express his readiness to overlook the matter, and forget what had occurred. (*PP* 30)

By these and similar means, the innocence and ignorance of these so-called savants – the members of a supposedly 'learned' society – provide a measure of the treacherous and cowardly behaviour that they repeatedly encounter in their spasmodic journeying from one fiasco to the next. The most distressing and progressively threatening discovery that the Pickwickians make is that the immorality and ruthlessness that they slowly learn to perceive for what they are are not manifestations of individual viciousness but extensions of the systematic corruptness of public life. At the time of the election at Eatanswill, they are not yet sufficiently enlightened to be able to share in the narrator's castigation of the hollowness of political discourse and the meaninglessness of electoral procedure. But when Pickwick is arrested in the breach of promise suit, they are exposed at first hand to the pomposity, vacuousness, and total lack of principle of the officers of the law.

Pickwick ends up in prison and becomes totally disillusioned. By this time, sarcasm is being employed without a trace of levity, and the narrator has dispensed with the weapon of simulated innocence in order to address himself directly to the reader. 'This is no fiction' (*PP* 565) Dickens feels urged to point out. But Pickwick does not actually go into prison until nearly the end of the book. Before that moment, he does not apprehend the nature of the relation between individual vice and the social order. He has spent his career in repeated attempts at the reformation of individual characters, during which time his tenders of kindness and tolerance have been met with cheating and ingratitude. The most conspicuous offender in this regard is, of course, the irrepressible Jingle. Jingle represents the most ceaselessly effective resurgence of the Blotton principle; it should really be thought of as the Jingle principle, if anything. He reintroduces time and again the note of disruption, of individual self-interest and of shrewdness; he has his finger on the pulse of society to an extent that makes him plausible in any of the roles he chooses to play. He even speaks in fragmentary inscriptions, or jingles rather – strings of nouns and adjectives – staccato deliveries almost totally devoid of verb forms. He is a master of disguise and deception, his every reappearance marked by a change of costume, but he is always recognizable to the reader by his language – the recklessness and irregularity of his speech patterns being complemented by the substance of his anecdotes, with their images of alarming fracture:

> 'Heads, heads – take care of your heads!' cried the loquacious stranger, as they came out under the low archway, which in those days formed the entrance to the coach-yard. 'Terrible place – dangerous work – other day – five children – mother – tall lady, eating sandwiches – forgot the arch – crash – knock – children look round – mother's head off – sandwich in her hand – no mouth to put it in – head of a family off – shocking, shocking!' (*PP* 25–6)

Jingle is a spirit of misrule; a figure of manic hilarity who disrupts all of Pickwick's carefully laid plans to introduce peace and harmony into the relations of those he encounters, and whose monstrous fictions amount to a wholesale rejection of other points of view, or of any point of view held in common – the world has reference only to himself. His is the retaliation of an embattled individuality prevented from earning a position of advantage in society, or a chance of self-definition, unless by usurpation and treachery, and in this he is a hyperbolized version of Blotton. Both are types of all those who lack the money that Pickwick has with which to construct a private world of their own, protected from the relentless depredations of public life. Outside the havens of eighteenth-century rural imperturbability and mutual dependence, like Dingly Dell, and the genteel utopia of the Pickwick Club, the world is an arena of opportunism and ferocious rivalry, whose tenor is most adequately rendered in the ever-present shadow of the interpolated stories. Jingle's resourcefulness is, accordingly, proportional to Mr Pickwick's simplicity, because Jingle has no other means of surviving in this world.

What is remarkable is how much, even when Jingle is not present in the narrative, the tone and method of the narration owe an allegiance to the confidence tricks, fraudulence even, exaggeration, and sheer ridiculousness of Jingle – it reproduces the same high-energy spurts of invention not clearly connected; it puts all its verve into constructions that steer triumphantly away from coherence. And on that score it would seem that the book is subject to irreconcilable impulses of enthusiasm for the transparent honesty of Pickwick, on the one hand, and for the outrageous deceptions of Jingle, on the other.

The narrative of events comes to show an irresistible attraction towards the repetition of personal encounters between these two men, so that Pickwick and Jingle come to seem like opposites to each other. However, there is a sense in which they share a bond of reaction to an existing state of affairs – a state of affairs that Jingle cheerfully assumes is unreclaimable, but that Pickwick strives to reclaim. They end up together in the Fleet Prison, after which Pickwick loses faith in the renovation of the social fabric as a whole and limits himself to a much smaller scale of philanthropic projections. Within this smaller scale, he effects the reformation (the supposed reformation, not the absolutely assured reformation) of Jingle, to whom he is reconciled by the experience of being a fellow-prisoner. From this point until the end of the book Pickwick's activity of setting things to rights is more effective, because more muted and realistic. But, irrespective of developments in the narrated sequence of events, the writing both before and after the episode of the Fleet Prison is organized by the need to affront gentility with rudeness, or to convert discord into harmony: to struggle with the competing demands for space of the Pickwick principle and the Jingle principle, out of a necessity either to evade or to palliate the pressure of social circumstance. Much of the comedy is in fact dependent on this dynamic complication. Good examples can be found on practically any page in chapter forty-eight, for instance, which comes after the Fleet Prison incident.

This particular chapter opens with Ben Allen and Bob Sawyer gloomily discussing Allen's sister, Arabella, whom they are agreed ought to be married off to Sawyer. They are unaware that she has already eloped with Mr Pickwick's protégé, Nathaniel Winkle. But the old lady who has suddenly drawn up outside in a private fly is aware; she is Ben Allen's aunt, and has come to break the news of the elopement to him as gently as she can. Her fly is driven by a 'surly-looking man' who evidently serves as factotum to the old lady, and whose appearance, together with the general appearance of the fly, testifies euphemistically to the fact that she is an 'old lady of economic habits'.

The evidently straitened circumstances in which she is forced to live have produced a revolution in the relations of mistress and servant. Martin, confident in the knowledge that his mistress cannot afford to dispense with his services, exploits the situation and usurps the position of dominance; which he proceeds to demonstrate with a spectacular inversion of the expected courtesy and attentiveness:

> 'Martin!' said the old lady, calling to the surly man, out of the front window.
>
> 'Well?' said the surly man, touching his hat to the old lady.
>
> 'Mr Sawyer's,' said the old lady.
>
> 'I was going there,' said the surly man.
>
> The old lady nodded the satisfaction which this proof of the surly man's foresight imparted to her feelings; and the surly man giving a smart lash to the chubby horse, they all repaired to Mr Bob Sawyer's together.
>
> 'Martin!' said the old lady, when the fly stopped at the door of Mr Robert Sawyer, late Nockemorf.

> 'Well?' said Martin.
>
> 'Ask the lad to step out, and mind the horse.'
>
> 'I'm going to mind the horse myself,' said Martin, laying his whip on the roof of the fly.
>
> 'I can't permit it, on any account,' said the old lady; 'your testimony will be very important, and I must take you into the house with me. You must not stir from my side during the whole interview. Do you hear?'
>
> 'I hear,' replied Martin.
>
> 'Well, what are you stopping for?'
>
> 'Nothing,' replied Martin. So saying, the surly man leisurely descended from the wheel, on which he had been poising himself on the tops of the toes of his right foot, and having summoned the boy in the grey livery, opened the coach-door, flung down the steps, and thrusting in a hand enveloped in a dark wash-leather glove, pulled out the old lady with as much unconcern in his manner as if she were a bandbox.
>
> 'Dear me!' exclaimed the old lady. 'I am so flurried, now I have got here, Martin, that I'm all in a tremble.' (*PP* 634–5)

Not only does Martin respond to his mistress's timid requests with a clipped boorishness, he even manhandles her with an ostentatious roughness. As much as he is unconcerned by any injury this might be doing to her feelings, so she is taken up with a concern to mollify him. She lives in a perpetual tremor of conciliations and fatuous appreciations, ignoring his downright rudeness and even interpreting it as evidence of a native wisdom: 'The old lady nodded the satisfaction which this proof of the surly man's foresight imparted to her feelings.' When he treats her like a physical object, she reacts ingenuously and in a confidential tone. It is a familiar pattern of a strictly defined social situation enhancing a self-serving proletarian opportunism in the face of a helpless and myopic attempt to preserve gentility.

The old lady then goes indoors and attempts to convey her message to Ben Allen through the medium of Bob Sawyer, who is precisely the wrong man to choose for the job, since he is likely to be even more shocked by the news than his friend. Sawyer, who does not know what is in store, thinks he is dealing with an anxious patient whose symptoms must be diagnosed. The suave and conciliatory tones that he employs in his professional capacity are turned into a violent shriek of indignation when he discovers the facts of the case. The old lady is only using him as a mediator because the delicacy of the matter is such that she is unsure how to proceed; but Sawyer, who mistakes her drift until the last moment, thinks all the time that he is diagnosing an illness, and counterposes to her delicacy his reductive and degrading verdict that 'The stomach is the cause'. When he relays the vital information to Allen abruptly – which is the reverse of the old lady's intention – the result is a totally spontaneous and irrational attack by Allen upon Martin and an ensuing scene of extraordinary mayhem:

> 'What!' said, or rather shouted, Mr Bob Sawyer.
>
> 'Married,' repeated the old lady.
>
> Mr Bob Sawyer stopped to hear no more; but darting from the surgery into the outer shop, cried in a stentorian voice, 'Ben, my boy, she's bolted!'
>
> Mr Ben Allen, who had been slumbering behind the counter, with his head half a foot or so below his knees, no sooner heard this appalling communication, than he made a precipitate rush at Mr Martin, and, twisting his hand in the neckcloth of that taciturn servitor, expressed an intention of choking him where he stood. This intention, with a promptitude often the effect of desperation, he at once commenced carrying into execution, with much vigour and surgical skill.
>
> Mr Martin, who was a man of few words and possessed but little power of eloquence or persuasion, submitted to this operation with a very calm and agreeable expression of countenance, for some seconds; finding, however, that it threatened speedily to lead to a result which would place it beyond his power to claim any wages, board or otherwise, in all time to come, he muttered an inarticulate remonstrance and felled Mr Benjamin Allen to the ground. As that gentleman had his hands entangled in his cravat, he had no alternative but to follow him to the floor. There they both lay struggling, when the shop door opened, and the party was increased by the arrival of two most unexpected visitors: to wit, Mr Pickwick, and Mr Samuel Weller. (*PP* 637)

The unleashing of physical violence becomes transformed into a brand of almost slapstick physical cavorting. But what the comedy really stems from is the way in which crudely physical action is expressed in such polished language. Instinctive movements are translated into rational processes, described as if they were the outcome of weighty deliberation. The split second in which Martin reacts to the attempt to throttle him with a shout and a blow is expanded in imagination into a sober reflection on his part on the prospective loss of what really motivates his life – the claiming of wages and board from the impoverished old lady (and for as little return as possible, one might add). What is chaotic and explosive in the action gets composed into order and even decorum in the language. It is, of course, a false order, just as futile as the undignified attempts of the combatants to overpower each other, but it is a version, in a humorous technique, of the same kind of unrealistic pacification of the violent and irrational that is constantly being essayed by Mr Pickwick, who arrives on the scene at the end of this passage, to carry on the process in his own terms.

Bob Sawyer and Ben Allen behave with such fury on learning of Arabella's elopement because their own freedom of manœuvre is severely limited by a chronic lack of funds. (Arabella is shortly to become an heiress.) The effect on Ben Allen of being told the identity of the successful suitor is to perform, almost ceremoniously, an action of great specificity: 'Mr Benjamin Allen deliberately crushed his spectacles beneath the heel of his boot, and having picked up the pieces, and put them into three separate pockets, folded his arms, bit his lips, and looked in a threatening manner at the bland features of Mr Pickwick' (*PP* 639). In this single act of destruction and restoration, fragmentation and rescue, we find the same impossible combination of recklessness and composure operating under the strain of social disability as is liable to emerge in so many other more extended and differently inflected moments of crisis in the text.

The coda to this particular passage entails Pickwick's dawning awareness that the old lady of 'economic habits' is 'evidently much struck by the mode in which he had advocated her niece's cause' (*PP* 641). In other words: she has taken due note of the fact that Pickwick has been recommending Winkle on grounds, among others, of his financial solvency, and has begun to conceive a matrimonial ambition of her own with her eye on the well-to-do Pickwick. Gentility prevents her from naming the price of her attentions, but the 'comforting' and 'strengthening' phrases she substitutes for her real motive are so vacuous that the reader is obviously intended to refer to what they have displaced: 'after all, perhaps it was well it was no worse; the least said the soonest mended... what was over couldn't be begun, and what couldn't be cured must be endured' (*PP* 641). These clichés of reparation and unification are merely irredeemably banal parodies of Pickwick's own belief in the powers of tolerance and kindness as a means of defeating rapacity and unrest. He flees from the scene in a cold sweat, just as he flees from every woman with the same object in view. But he does not bolt because he has been made to realize that he is face to face with a perversion of his own disarming tactics; he bolts from women, just as he bolts from reality in general, because he is unable to contemplate the idea of a close relationship with a real woman, who might bring him real children, and who might be part of an extended family that would give him real relations. He finds his happiness in providing for himself surrogates of all these, in composing an artificial family whose members he has selected. Real families in the novel are more often than not sources of unnatural behaviour, of treachery: and are sometimes even death traps. Especially in the interpolated tales, where parents turn against children and vice versa; where husbands are capable of hounding wives to death. Pickwick finds himself in the world of the interpolated tales, or at least he walks into a characteristic setting when he enters the Fleet Prison at a crucial juncture in the book.

Dickens makes a personal appearance at this point – he thrusts himself into prominence with a direct address to the reader making it clear that many of the prisoners are able to survive only by virtue of the random benevolence of passers-by, and he refers to the institutionalized corruptness of 'the just and wholesome law which declares that the sturdy felon shall be fed and clothed, [while] the penniless debtor shall be left to die of starvation and nakedness' (*PP* 565). 'This is no fiction', he points out, but it *is* coextensive with the world of the fiction that extends, before and after, beyond the scope of this episode. The random effects of Pickwickian benevolence are virtually meaningless in the context of a world whose overall pattern is one in which such behaviour can only ever be interpreted as freakish and unreliable.

The narrator then records Pickwick's general reactions of shock and indignation at the scene that presents itself, before rendering his discovery that one of the prisoners is Jingle:

> Mr Pickwick gradually worked himself to the boiling-over point; and so excited was he with his reflections on this subject, that he had

> burst into the room to which he had been directed, before he had any distinct recollection, either of the place in which he was, or of the object of his visit.
>
> The general aspect of the room recalled him to himself at once; but he had no sooner cast his eyes on the figure of a man who was brooding over the dusty fire, than, letting his hat fall on the floor, he stood perfectly fixed, and immoveable, with astonishment.
>
> Yes; in tattered garments, and without a coat; his common calico shirt, yellow and in rags; his hair hanging over his face; his features changed with suffering, and pinched with famine; there sat Mr Alfred Jingle: his head resting on his hand, his eyes fixed upon the fire, and his whole appearance denoting misery and dejection. (*PP* 565–6)

What is immediately striking is the extent to which Jingle is made almost unrecognizable. He usually bursts into the action with an instantly available virtuosity, his speeches careering through their material at a frenzied pace. But here he is presented through the medium of a syntax that is hobbled, repetitious, lifeless, unvaried. There is only one active verb, and even that has a paradoxically passive effect, since it delivers the information that Jingle 'sat'. Whereas, when the narration has been inspired by Jingle, it has been infected by his energy almost in a spirit of truancy, or of the enjoyment of a somehow illegitimate pleasure, here the sympathetic identification with the pathos of his situation is unmodified by any, even vaguely, moral filter. It is, of course, appropriate to recall the burden of affect that Dickens carried round with him for the whole of his life in respect of the conditions in a debtor's prison, because he had suffered the trauma of his own father's incarceration in one. So it seems significant that Jingle, the liar by definition, who has totally jettisoned all moral responsibility towards others, should be judged so much less harshly than the punitive agency that drains him of his very life force. Jingle is only one in a succession of prisoners who are portrayed as being enclosed in the destructive isolation of their own either insane or despairing preoccupations. But this condition is only an exacerbation of the friendlessness of the outside world, a logical extension of the outcome of involvement in a society where personal ties are controlled by insincerity and aggression; which can only be coped with by deciding to play according to its sordid rules, or which can be rejected by means of voluntary withdrawal. The latter option is not open to Jingle, since to someone in his social position it is equal to an obliteration of the self. Mr Pickwick is in a different social position, which is why he can afford to undergo voluntarily the isolation that is enforced upon prisoners like Jingle. He withdraws from the society that allows Mrs Bardle to bring the breach of promise suit against him by electing to go to prison rather than pay bail. Once inside the prison, and sickened by the panorama of degradation it displays, he withdraws even further: 'I have seen enough,' he announces, 'Henceforth I will be a prisoner in my own room.'

This is what the programme of *The Pickwick Papers* has shrunk to. The ambition announced in the prospectus of being exposed to and assimilating all the variousness of the world – of 'carrying... speculation... into a wider field... [of] extending... travels [and of] enlarging [the] sphere of observation' (*PP* 15); of endless motion and employment and of eagerness to record the views of other men – is transformed into a need for the stillness and silence and blankness that can be found within the four walls of a prison room. And even when Pickwick leaves prison, he withdraws: he goes on no further travels but chooses the seclusion of 'peaceful retirement'. The end of the novel is bathed in the restorative light of the patronage Pickwick extends to the friends he surrounds himself with. And this time there is no comic deflation of his centrality in this sphere, as there was at the start of the book. The admiring tones of the narration do not allow for the slightest margin of dissent from the exemplary candour of Pickwick himself, and the novel ends as a celebration of the way in which Pickwick is able to settle his affairs.

But his settlement is an utopian one, the fulfilment of a private fantasy, and with it he loses all hold of the public world. There is nothing already existing in the entire fabric of English social life that can provide him with a foundation to build on. Dingly Dell is only a quaint enclosure of mythologized England, hived off from the instabilities of the real world, and no longer in significant contact with its rural predecessors in the world of the eighteenth-century novel, whose function was to be there all the time, waiting to be rediscovered. Pickwick's immersion in English village life has revealed a milder form of the competitiveness that has so shattered him in the urban context; and its essential pettiness is affectionately but relentlessly exposed in the aggrandized exploits of rival cricket teams, whose supporters vie with one another as if the issues at stake were ethical cruxes.

In narrative terms, the repeated collision of separate purposes represented typically by Pickwick and Jingle is not resolved but defused by the Prison scene, which also demonstrates in what ways those two figures might be associated with each other rather than held apart, and conveys the extent to which both are conditioned by an awareness of an unmanageably unjust social world. The only alternative outcomes are defeat or unreality, and it is not surprising that Dickens should choose unreality. But if there is any value in the demonstration that something like the same complication of forces recurs in terms of character, action, imagery, setting, style, and comic technique, then worrying too much about the amalgamation of many different narratives into one may look somewhat beside the point.

Of course, there is a biographical reference, and perhaps a psychoanalytical reference, to be disclosed in all of this, in connection with the way that Pickwick's relationship with Sam Weller – and for that matter, Tony Weller's relationship with Sam Weller – can be seen as redemptive of the filial relationship that Dickens suffered from with regard to his own father and which is perhaps only adequately borne witness to in the violence and mistrust of the interpolated tales.

But what I prefer to adduce as the most important context for the kind of reading I have given of *The Pickwick Papers* is the fact that it was written in the aftermath of the failure of the 1832 Reform Bill; it was written in a period of mistrust, of renewed scepticism about institutional change, when political and legal discourses had had time to reappear as inadequate, as not working properly. Dickens's own experience as a reporter would have confirmed the extent to which the political and legal languages – the official languages – of British culture involved a distortion and a betrayal of the needs of the British people. Dickens's passionate disillusionment in this regard is nowhere more evident than in the next few novels he wrote, centring on the predicament, and the moral abandonment, of the British child.

2

The Image of the Child

OLIVER TWIST, NICHOLAS NICKLEBY, THE OLD CURIOSITY SHOP, DOMBEY AND SON

Probably the most famous scene in *Oliver Twist* (1838), perhaps one of the most well-known scenes in all of Dickens's works, is the one in which Oliver asks for more. In the popular imagination this is a novel associated with the idea of going hungry. Which means that there is a special significance to be attached to any subsequent scene in which Oliver states he does not need any more, because he is no longer hungry. There is one occasion on which he is directly asked whether he is hungry or not, when his emphatic answer is 'No' (*OT* 126). This is during his convalescent period after first arriving at Mr Brownlow's house. His interlocutor is a doctor, who has quite correctly diagnosed at least one important contributing factor to Oliver's physical weakness. *Oliver Twist* was written during a period when the medical profession, and in particular the *Lancet,* was at the forefront of attacks on the Poor Law Commissioners over their refusal to attribute the high mortality rates in the workhouses to the inadequate diet offered to the inmates.[1] Oliver's well-being is guaranteed once he has arrived in a house where the debate about nutritional values focuses on the relative merits of 'beautiful strong broth' and port wine (*OT* 130), rather than on the relative merits of giving meat to paupers or witholding it, which is where the issue lies for Mr Bumble (*OT* 93).

But Oliver's residence with Brownlow is interrupted, and after his abduction by Sikes and Nancy he is returned to the way of life and dietary habits of the lower classes. It is actually while he is in the Sikes/Nancy household, on the evening before the expedition to Chertsey, that his appetite falls off again, not this time because he has been well fed, but from aversion. This is when the main meal of the day takes the form of a dish of sheeps' heads (*OT* 201). The sheep's head was a recognized meal during the nineteenth century, but it would have been unusual in an urban working-class household, where the staple diet consisted of bread, potatoes, and tea. Oliver is not squeamish over his food, having consumed without hesitation a plate of 'bits' originally intended for the Sowerberrys' dog (*OT* 74). Why does Dickens fix on sheeps' heads for the meal over which Oliver's appetite hesitates?

The eating of heads is actually fairly widespread in the text of *Oliver Twist*; or at least it is constantly alluded to, in the form of Grimwig's comical threats to eat his own, in the event of his being proved wrong. At one level, Grimwig's slogan is a harmless eccentricity, but at another level, it evokes an extremely disturbing image. If the humour acts primarily as a means of toning down the virulence of this imagery, it is not clear how effectively it works. Grimwig's fantasy of self-mutilation is too close for comfort to the actual damage inflicted on himself by the epileptic Monks; as Nancy reports, 'His lips are often discoloured and disfigured with the marks of teeth; for he has desperate fits, and sometimes even bites his hands and covers them with wounds' (*OT* 413). This abstracted gnawing at one's own body is reflected shortly afterwards in the behaviour of Fagin, waiting in an agony of suspense for the arrival of Bill Sikes: 'His right hand was raised to his lips, and as absorbed in thought, he bit his long black nails, he disclosed among his toothless gums a few such fangs as should have been a dog's or rat's' (*OT* 417). Devouring the self is the expression of a bestial nature; as the case of Monks makes clear, it results from a complete loss of self-possession, and the description of Fagin identifies this with subhuman forms of existence. With both men, violence against the self diverts an aggressive energy more often directed outwards at others, and usually expressed in terms of damage to the head or neck. Fagin's resentment of Bolter (Noah Claypole) is transformed into a hysterical desire to cut his head off: 'Bolter's throat, Bill; never mind the girl – Bolter's throat as deep as you can cut. Saw his head off!' (*OT*

472). Bolter speaks too much – he is a lifelong informer – but, as his name suggests, he also poses a threat with his voracious appetite, which Fagin regards as competition for his own means of subsistence. When Nancy switches her allegiance from Fagin to Oliver, shortly after having helped the former to kidnap the latter, she does so in order to prevent a similar kind of injury being inflicted on the boy; specifically, to ensure 'the child shan't be torn down by the dog' (*OT* 164), the dog having been previously described as eying Oliver 'as if he were anxious to attach himself to his windpipe without delay' (*OT* 159).

Mr Grimwig's bark is worse than his bite; his grimness can be removed as easily as a wig (although a wig is uncomfortably close to a representation of the entire head). He seems remote from the bestial savagery of a character like Fagin; but the difference between his fantasies of violence and those of Fagin depends ultimately on a difference in tone and relative intensity. The criminal characters are not the only ones prone to vindictiveness and an impulse to predatory behaviour. When Fagin is finally cornered, it is actually the women in the crowd who 'swore they'd tear his heart out!' (*OT* 445). Oliver is chased by a crowd, in the belief that he has stolen Brownlow's pocket handkerchief, and the pursuit of this 'one wretched breathless child' drives the posse of adults into a frenzy: 'and as they follow on his track, and gain upon him every instant, they hail his decreasing strength with still louder shouts, and whoop and scream with joy' (*OT* 116). The narrator accounts for this mass hysteria in terms of a universal tendency to eat or be eaten: 'There is a passion *for hunting something* deeply implanted in the human breast' (*OT* 116). There are no significant differences in the behaviour of the two crowds who chase Oliver, who is innocent, and Sikes, who is guilty. The first chase ends in a blow to Oliver's face, the second in the breaking of Sikes's neck.

But this collective abandonment of self-restraint is one thing; an individual loss of self-control is another. Monks provides the most spectacular instance of involuntary violence, but an unpredictable loss of mental balance, and sometimes of consciousness, is found in a wide range of other characters. Nancy's behaviour, after her attempt to preserve Oliver from attack, shows a rapid deterioration in the instinct of self-preservation; she begins by laughing hysterically, then bites her own lips into a bloody state (another version of head-eating), and eventually tears at her hair and dress 'in a transport of passion' (*OT* 167) until she faints. But as with the universal passion for hunting, the loss of self-government afflicts the law-abiding as well as the criminal classes. Brownlow and Losberne, in their impatience to 'avenge' the murdered Nancy, set off in pursuit of the culprits 'each in a fever of excitement wholly uncontrollable' (*OT* 441). Losberne and Grimwig are frequently characterized as impetuous and inconsistent, while it is actually in his initial encounter with the law in the shape of the magistrate that Brownlow is revealed as a man barely able to contain his passions: 'in a perfect frenzy of rage and defiance' (*OT* 124). The savage irrationality of the magistrate's conduct is confirmed by his name, Fang, which recalls the analogy between Fagin's teeth and the teeth of dogs and rats (Fang is almost an anagram of Fagin). The barrier between civilized and uncivilized behaviour is overstepped by virtually every kind of character, and the inefficacy of this barrier is brought out most vividly in the recurrent crisis of self-regulation.

The most profound failure to organize one's experience and impose order on it is suggested by an inability to distinguish dreams from reality, or a sleeping from a waking state. Oliver undergoes one of the most dramatic examples of this semi-conscious condition when he is spied on by Monks and Fagin at the Maylies' cottage window. Rose Maylie herself is overpowered by her first interview with Nancy because it has 'more the semblance of a rapid dream than an actual occurrence' (*OT* 366). Sikes's wanderings after the death of Nancy provide the occasion for the most protracted version of this delusive state, while the most intense and destabilizing such experience is probably that of Fagin, sitting in the condemned cell, 'awake, but dreaming' (*OT* 470). Again, the loss of control and orientation is a circumstance all the characters are liable to, irrespective of class or personality.

Perhaps the most confusing source of these confusions is the kind of Wordsworthian vision that the text quite overtly regards as the index and guarantee of Oliver's essential goodness. Born and brought up in the brutalizing and systematically unjust environment of the workhouse, Oliver's only chance of acquiring his moral bearings is through insertion in the Wordsworthian tradition of the child 'trailing clouds of glory', closer to God than the adult, because closer to the moment of birth, which inaugurates a process of 'forgetting' God's glory. Dickens's version of this emphasis is organized around the notion of a dream that crosses the threshold between sleeping and waking states:

> The boy stirred, and smiled in his sleep, as though these marks of pity and compassion had awakened some pleasant dream of a love and affection he had never known. Thus, a strain of gentle music, or the rippling of water in a silent place, or the odour of a flower, or the mention of a familiar word, will sometimes call up sudden dim remembrances of scenes that never were, in this life; which vanish like a breath; which some brief memory of a happier existence, long gone by, would seem to have awakened; which no voluntary exertion of the mind can ever recall. (*OT* 268)

The conceptual framework provided by sleeping, waking, dreaming, remembering, and forgetting might have been borrowed direct from Wordsworth (for example, 'Ode: Intimations of Immortality'), but it creates a problematical ambiguity in the text. Dickens relies on the cultural authority of the Wordsworthian child to account for Oliver's abiding innocence and rectitude; and this authority is recognized ultimately even by Mr Bumble, who tries, humorously of course, to improve on the Wordsworthian dictum 'the child is father to the man': 'I always loved that boy as if he'd been my – my – my own grandfather' (*OT* 460). The problem with the Wordsworthian apparatus is that it gives a positive value to the erosion of a boundary between dreaming and waking that is otherwise given a disturbing or unnerving effect.

The most haunting of these 'waking dreams' are those that feature the experience of being stared at. The uneasiness this produces is a feeling shared by innocent and guilty, rich and poor alike. At one crucial moment in the slowly dawning realization of the nature of his connection with Oliver, Mr Brownlow calls up 'before his mind's eye a vast amphitheatre of faces... of friends, and foes, and of many that had been almost strangers peering intrusively from the crowd' (*OT* 119). The resemblance between Oliver's face and one of the faces in his mind's eye is what he has difficulty coming to terms with: 'No,' said the old gentleman, shaking his head; 'it must be imagination'. Oliver himself is similarly mesmerized by the face in the portrait: 'the eyes look so sorrowful; and where I sit, they seem fixed upon me' (*OT* 129); and, although Mrs Bedwin wheels his chair into a position from which he cannot actually see the painting, in his imagination the details of the apparently staring face remain just as vivid to him: 'Oliver *did* see it in his mind's eye as distinctly as if he had not altered his position' (*OT* 129). The 'amphitheatre' of Brownlow's imagination actually resembles very closely the 'firmament' of Fagin's: the hostile crowd of onlookers who fill the court during Fagin's trial: 'The court was paved, from floor to roof, with human faces. Inquisitive and eager eyes peered from every inch of space... he seemed to stand surrounded by a firmament, all bright with gleaming eyes' (*OT* 466).

The vague discomposure suffered by Brownlow and Oliver is transformed into an agonizing sense of exposure in Fagin's case, but even his failure to escape the ubiquitous gaze does not keep pace with Sikes's inability to stop himself seeing the eyes of Nancy wherever he looks: 'Those widely staring eyes, so lustreless and so glassy, that he had better borne to see than think upon them, appeared in the midst of the darkness; light in themselves, but giving light to nothing. There were but two, but they were everywhere' (*OT* 428–9). In this instance of the waking dream, it is clearly the 'mind's eye' that creates a greater sense of oppression than empirical observation. For both Sikes and Fagin, the eyes staring at them are punitive, at least by implication; they either anticipate, or participate in, the formal procedures of the law. Mr Brownlow invokes the 'eye of the law', which elicits one of Bumble's most celebrated protests: 'the law is a ass – a idiot. If that's the eye of the law, the law is a bachelor; and the worst I wish the law is, that his eye may be opened by experience – by experience'(*OT* 462).

It is not obviously the law, but Brownlow, who is the bachelor, and it is his solitude that is accentuated by the crowd of faces that populate his memory. What all the staring faces in the book have in common is a tendency to single out the individuals they observe, or who imagine them. Being stared at is an essentially isolating experience. It corresponds to a widespread fear of being alone that is particularly acute in precisely those figures who are already marginalized. Monks is a striking example of a character without any security of position in society, who 'appeared to entertain an invincible repugnance to being left alone' (*OT* 344). A similar anxiety after Nancy's murder is what impels Sikes to take part in the firefighting; it offers him a temporary experience of community, of collective effort, to shelter behind. Probably the most desolate experience, though, is that of Fagin, whose race and culture, as well as his lack of companionship, leave him intensely isolated during his period in the condemned cell. But the most protracted experience of loneliness is, of course, that of Oliver, and of the thousands of orphans like him. There is no sense in which marginalization and friendlessness are simply the just deserts of those who put themselves beyond the law or the pale of decency; they are equally well the afflictions of those whom the state has no interest in reclaiming and whom society ignores. It is only through Brownlow's project of forming a 'little society' that certain of the individuals in the story can be brought into relations of mutual affection and dependence. Mutuality is a seminal concept in all of Dickens's works; but its reach is limited. The emphasis on 'little' is almost an admission of British society's failure on a grander scale. It is not just that Britain is unamenable to reform; it is rather that its laws and social attitudes positively militate against the creation and maintenance of genuine community values. It includes Bates, but equally well includes Claypole; it destroys Sikes and Fagin, but equally well abandons Nancy to destruction; it rescues Oliver, but resigns itself to the loss of Dick. And in the final redemption of Agnes Fleming, it tries to make up for the mistakes of the past, but in a way that deflects attention away from the likelihood that all the same mistakes will be made in the future. What the laws of England ensure, in fact, what the Poor Law of 1834 guarantees, is that all of the other alphabetically named paupers apart from Oliver will necessarily go on asking for more.

One of the most crucial areas in need of reform in the 1830s was the schooling system, and it is this context for Victorian childhood that comes under Dickens's scrutiny in his novel of 1838–9, *Nicholas Nickleby*. Probably the most notorious of Dickens's educational establishments, Dotheboys Hall, with its headmaster Wackford Squeers, goes through a show of instructing its pupils as a mere pretext for exploiting their labour:

> 'Third boy, what's a horse?'
> 'A beast, sir,' replied the boy.
> 'So it is,' said Squeers. 'Ain't it Nickleby?'
> 'I believe there is no doubt of that, sir,' answered Nicholas.
> 'Of course there isn't,' said Squeers. 'A horse is a quadruped, and quadruped's Latin for beast, as everybody that's gone through the grammar knows, or else where's the use of having grammars at all?'
> 'Where, indeed!' said Nicholas abstractedly.
> 'As you're perfect in that,' resumed Squeers, turning to the boy, 'go and look after *my* horse, and rub him down well, or I'll rub you down. The rest of the class go and draw water up till somebody tells you to leave off, for it's washing day tomorrow, and they want the coppers filled.' (*NN* 100–1)

The second injunction, to fill the coppers, is arguably less educationally damaging than the first, which entails mistranslating Latin into English. Squeers's systematic corruptions of language stem from ignorance, but they epitomize the duplicity of an educational system that undermines the value of social relations by perverting all the key value words for ties of affection and obligation. For those of Squeers's pupils who survive, education is an education in hypocrisy, a prolonged exposure to moral confusion that paradoxically sharpens their own sense of the double standards of those in power. As Charles Cheeryble points out with reference to Smike, the Dotheboys regime constitutes a linguistic aversion therapy, which leads in the end to the pupils setting their own instincts against convention:

> 'Here is a poor lad who has never felt a parent's care, who has scarcely known anything all his life but suffering and sorrow, presented to a man who he is told is his father, and whose first act is to signify his intention of putting an end to his short term of happiness: of consigning him to his old fate, and taking him from the only friend he has ever had – which is yourself. If Nature, in such a case, put into that lad's breast but one secret prompting which urged him towards his father and away from you, she would be a liar and an idiot.' (*NN* 563)

The problem is that there is nothing more natural than an idiot – indeed the word 'natural' was in common use to describe an idiot; Smike himself is an idiot, or at least a simpleton. Dickens perceives correctly that words like 'Nature' are particularly susceptible to capture by convention, yet he both diagnoses the semantic slipperiness that results and makes use of it himself. The quality of Smike's yearning for Nicholas is such as to complicate still further the question of what is regarded as 'natural' or 'unnatural' behaviour. Cheeryble assumes that Smike is endowed with a moral instinct, but other instincts may be at work; the strength of the boy's attachment to Nicholas is diminished to the extent that Dickens finds him another love interest shortly before his death. With the extraordinary intensity of his affections diverted to a more conventional object, Smike is allowed to die. But the new object is Nicholas's own sister, and Smike dies in his arms not hers, finally happy in the receipt of Nicholas's kiss.

The revolt of instinct against oppression may have morality on its side, but it may also be a prompting with secrets of its own. One of the most interesting episodes in this novel concerns the explosion of protest at Dotheboys Hall, following the downfall of Squeers. The boys rise in one body to revenge themselves on the remaining members of the Squeers family. Dickens makes it clear that their crescendo of violence is about to become irreversibly destructive when John Browdie arrives just in time to restrain them. The boys' hysterical abandon is partly attributable to their sensing that the hated regime is the only social structure they have any experience of, so that their frenzy of rage is both an avowal and a denial of their utter dependence on it. The sequel to their little revolution includes a pathetic demonstration of the boys' fear of freedom:

> There were a few timid young children, who, miserable as they had been, and many as were the tears they had shed in the wretched school, still knew no other home, and had formed for it a sort of attachment, which made them weep when the bolder spirits fled, and cling to it as a refuge. Of these, some were found crying under hedges and in such places, frightened at the solitude. One had a dead bird in a little cage; he had wandered nearly twenty miles, and when his poor favourite died, lost courage, and lay down beside him. Another was discovered in a yard hard by the school, sleeping with a dog, who bit at those who came to remove him, and licked the sleeping child's pale face. (*NN* 773–4)

This form of vulnerability haunted Dickens; he wrote eloquently in *Barnaby Rudge* and *A Tale of Two Cities* about freed prisoners pining for the conditions they had known in jail. The idea of children exhibiting this pattern of behaviour as if it were second nature to them obviously moved him greatly. Their seeking-out the companionship and even the protection of dumb animals, since they cannot conceive of finding either among humans, means yet another adjustment of the reader's understanding of 'Nature', and of what counts as 'natural'.

Perhaps the most controversial image of the child in Dickens's early work is provided by the figure of Little Nell in *The Old Curiosity Shop* (1840–1). The excessive idealizing of this central character dominates the representations of children in the book. Nell's angelic purity is echoed in the sanctity of the old schoolmaster's favourite pupil in chapter 25, but such mutually reinforcing portrayals do not prevent altogether the imagining of other conditions in childhood. Alternative modes of behaviour are embodied in characters such as Kit Nubbles and Barbara, Tom Scott and Jacob, the poor apprentice Miss Edwards and her sister. The most extraordinary case of all, one that offers both a parallel and a contrast to the situation of Nell, is that of the Marchioness.

The Marchioness is a victim of the same kind of dietary system that Oliver Twist protests against. The physical abuse and psychological intimidation practised by Sally Brass revolve around a daily ritual intended to make the half-starved child responsible for her own state of malnourishment:

> 'Are you there?' said Miss Sally.
>
> 'Yes, ma'am,' was the answer in a weak voice.
>
> 'Go further away from the leg of mutton, or you'll be picking it, I know,' said Miss Sally.
>
> The girl withdrew into a corner, while Miss Brass took a key from her pocket, and opening the safe, brought from it a dreary waste of cold potatoes, looking as eatable as Stonehenge. This she placed before the small servant, ordering her to sit down before it, and then, taking up a great carving-knife, made a mighty show of sharpening it upon the carving-fork.
>
> 'Do you see this?' said Miss Brass, slicing off about two square inches of cold mutton, after all this preparation, and holding it out on the point of the fork.

> The small servant looked hard enough at it with her hungry eyes to see every shred of it, small as it was, and answered, 'yes'.
>
> 'Then don't you ever go and say', retorted Miss Sally, 'that you hadn't meat here. There, eat it up.'
>
> This was soon done. 'Now, do you want any more?' said Miss Sally.
>
> The hungry creature answered with a faint 'No'. They were evidently going through an established form.
>
> 'You've been helped once to meat,' said Miss Brass, summing up the facts; 'you have had as much as you can eat, you're asked if you want any more, and you answer, "no!" Then don't you ever go and say you were allowanced, mind that.' (*OCS* 351)

Sally is rehearsing the terms of an official inquiry, constructing a case that would stand up in a court of law; she maintains her control over the Marchioness through a system of deprivation that ensures the child's own complicity, from a legal point of view, in the process. As the moving spirit in her brother's legal business, Sally epitomizes the degradation of official languages as these are used to justify the balance of power in normal social relations. The Marchioness is by far the most defenceless child in the book; she is certainly more isolated than Nell, and her movements are much more restricted. It is remarkable that her rescue comes about through the agency of Swiveller, since this puts her on an equal footing with Nell as an alternative sexual partner for him. Swiveller begins the novel as a potential husband for Nell and ends it by marrying the Marchioness; he swivels between these two object choices, both of whom are under age. In the opening scenes of the book, Nell is frequently the subject of male speculation, chiefly of a sexual nature. She figures in her own brother's manœuvring to marry her off to his biddable friend; even more disagreeably, she is asked to imagine herself as a future partner for Quilp: '"To be Mrs Quilp the second, when Mrs Quilp the first is dead, sweet Nell," said Quilp, wrinkling up his eyes and luring her towards him with his bent forefinger' (*OCS* 93). Small wonder that Nell takes fright at these phallic invitations; the ostensible reason for her taking to the road is to remove her grandfather from temptation, to end his enthralment to gambling, but another outcome of their truancy is to remove Nell from the scene where she is perceived as a sexual being.

She takes to the road with an elderly relative who should be well past the age of sexual activity, in a culture in which the condition of extreme old age is represented as a form of second childhood: the post-sexual and the pre-sexual become equivalent. The denouement of the novel reunites the grandfather with his long-lost brother, who employs the complex syntax of rational maturity to propose that the two of them are actually becoming infantile, regressing happily to 'set up our rest again among our boyish haunts; and going home with no hope realised, that had its growth in manhood – carrying back nothing that we brought away, but our old yearnings to each other – saving no fragment from the wreck of life, but that which first endeared it – may be indeed but children as at first' (*OCS* 652). Behind this prospect of restitution is a history of passionate division, of a lifelong separation occasioned by sexual rivalry; the innocuousness of old age is wished for against a background of conflicting desires so powerful that even the senile are capable of being reanimated by some version of them. When Nell's bedroom is broken into at night by a figure she does not initially know to be her grandfather, the description of his theft of her money is prefaced by a passage of writing that could be employed equally well in an account of sexual interference:

> A figure was there. Yes, she had drawn up the blind to admit the light when it should dawn, and there, between the foot of the bed and the dark casement, it crouched and slunk along, groping its way with noiseless hands, and stealing round the bed. She had no voice to cry for help, no power to move, but lay still, watching it.
>
> On it came – on, silently and stealthily, to the bed's head. The breath so near her pillow, that she shrunk back into it, lest those wandering hands should light upon her face. (*OCS* 301)

The grandfather needs her money to feed his obsession with gambling; it is gambling that transforms his behaviour utterly, bringing him alive with a passionate intensity expressed in a range of symptoms of bodily excitement. Gambling becomes a means of representing a complete loss of self-control, physical and psychological, that would otherwise be given an erotic motivation. Dick's courtship of the Marchioness begins with a game of cribbage in which the stake consists of two sixpences; the development of the relationship between this adult and minor involves a delicate negotiation between degrees of control and abandonment, a negotiation that is maintained subsequently throughout the entirety of their married life: 'And they played many hundred thousand games of cribbage together' (*OCS* 669).

Nell's own life centres on a chronic struggle for control: control over circumstances in which others pose a sexual threat to her; and control over herself, over her susceptibility to passionate imaginings, fantasies of encroachment and molestation. Her greatest fear is that her grandfather 'should kill himself and his blood come creeping, creeping, on the ground to her own bed-room door' (*OCS* 121). This fantasy of invasion by a man who has committed the ultimate act of self-abandonment is 'too terrible to dwell upon'; and Nell's subsequent career as exegete, both at Jarley's waxworks and at the village church, is designed to explain away the creatures of her imagination by surrounding herself with figures whose terrible histories can be rationalized and, following the cue of Mr Garland's bachelor brother, bowdlerized. While still in London, surrounded by suitors however unlikely, Nell 'fancied ugly faces that were frowning over at her and trying to peer into the room' (*OCS* 121); while in the provinces, surrounded by wax figures or tombs, Nell imposes her control over the characters she has to conjure up for others, reducing them to order through a mastery of narration.

This work of the imagination is an anaesthetizing process, which quells fear but which renders the subject immune to every kind of passion besides, making it inevitable that the story should culminate with the death of Nell, not simply for the sake of manipulating the plot, but because the character is bound to a project of repression so extreme that the logical outcome is self-negation, bringing out the potential embedded in the homonym of the character's name, (death) *knell*. There is a counterpart to her anaesthetizing self-control in the extraordinary endurance tests that Quilp subjects himself to. As diminutive as a child, and nowhere as unguarded as he is in his relationship with the boy Tom Scott, Quilp provides an opportunity for Dickens to pursue imaginatively the fundamental amorality of children. Like Nell, Quilp gives notice of his capacity for mastery by spectacular feats of self-control – which in his case means drinking a variety of boiling liquids without turning a hair. This indifference to physical discomfort converts into a form of bravado, the self-martyring tendency which Nell exemplifies with her cut and bruised feet, vividly echoed by the Marchioness losing one of her shoes during her fearful journey through the streets of London. Quilp's 'system' of desensitization is held in an impossible tension with moments of an almost ecstatic loss of restraint: 'Daniel Quilp withdrew into a dismantled skittle-ground behind the public-house, and, throwing himself upon the ground, actually screamed and rolled about in the most uncontrollable delight' (*OCS* 227). If maturity is recognized in an ability to regulate the self, Quilp's oscillating between extremes of control and abandon represents an excessive degree of childishness. Nell's method of subduing her fears through description and interpretation is contrasted strikingly with Quilp's treatment of the ship's figurehead, which serves him as the waxworks serve her; the figurehead is a gigantic object, which towers over Quilp like the voodoo doll of an adult (he identifies it with the self-possessed figure of Kit), eliciting neither detachment nor perspective but an inventive variety of physical assaults. Nell gravitates towards the acceptably anaemic condition of 'the Good Angel of the race' (*OCS* 637), while Quilp is alternately bestial and demonic; one is entombed, commemorated, and sanctified, the other is discarded and degraded in death; but neither qualifies for survival in the adult world of regulated appetites.

Nell's precise moment of death is not captured; the fact that she has died is established by a group of men converging on the room in which she sleeps. The pathos of child mortality is rendered through the expression of sentimental regret on the part of the elderly. The major difference between this scene and the death of Paul in *Dombey and Son* (1844–6) is that the later book explores the point of view of the child himself, as he comes to terms with the sentimentalism of the bereaved, well in advance of the actual event. There is a double irony at work in the record of Paul's reflections on the behaviour of those who clearly anticipate his deterioration, and in the record of his growing absorption in the imagery of river and sea. His unconsciousness of the real meaning behind the many sympathetic glances and speeches he receives, and his unawareness of the literary symbolism that his water imagery entails, appeal directly to the sentimentality of the reader by giving the reader responsibility for controlling the flow of sentiment.

But there is an interesting blind spot in Paul's insouciance, an obstruction in the way of his steady progress towards resignation, and that is the strange illegibility of his father's reaction to his decline. Mr Dombey becomes physically obscure to him in a way that no one else shares, a shadowy figure he cannot even identify:

> But the figure with its head upon its hand returned so often, and remained so long, and sat so still and solemn, that Paul began to wonder languidly, if it were real; and in the night-time saw it sitting there, with fear.
>
> 'Floy!' he said. 'What *is* that?'
>
> 'Where, dearest?'
>
> 'There! at the bottom of the bed.'
>
> 'There's nothing there, except Papa!'
>
> The figure lifted up its head, and rose, and coming to the bedside, said:
>
> 'My own boy! Don't you know me?'
>
> Paul looked it in the face, and thought, was this his father? But the face so altered to his thinking, thrilled while he gazed, as if it were in pain; and before he could reach out both his hands to take it between them, and draw it towards him, the figure turned away quickly from the little bed, and went out at the door. (*DS* 294)

Paul does not manage to draw his father into the scenario that the remaining characters participate in. He loses the chance of contact and fails to bid him goodbye, although he manages a series of goodbyes to others. His last words to Mr Dombey refer in fact to another character, Walter, in whom he seems more interested. What Mr Dombey remains outside of is a drawing-together of conventional literary properties, a stereotypical Victorian deathbed scene, which projects an image of childhood whose primary purpose is one of moral edification. As with his previous attempts to define the specificities of childhood experience, Dickens plays up to the expectations of his audience in a way that increases the tension between ideological construct and what that construct leaves in the shadows. The unspeakable and unspoken grief of Mr Dombey has the immediacy of a sensation – of a painful thrill – that cannot be represented as sentiment; it hovers like an apparition, like a spectre of loss and denial, whose unfinished business is what haunts the Dickensian image of childhood.

3

Authority and Rebellion

BARNABY RUDGE, AMERICAN NOTES FOR GENERAL CIRCULATION, MARTIN CHUZZLEWIT, HARD TIMES

There can be few novels that announce as many of their themes and concerns on the first page as *Barnaby Rudge* (1841) does. The first chapter sets the scene at an inn called *The Maypole* whose distance of twelve miles from London is measured from the Standard in Cornhill. The description of the inn, its landlord, and regulars conjures up a very conservative image of English traditions and history. Its chief claim to fame revolves around a visit of Elizabeth I culminating in a display of royal authority. And yet the name, *The Maypole,* evokes a very different tradition, that of the carnivalesque; and Cornhill was the location of the oldest and best-known maypole in England, notorious as the venue for Mayday rioting by the volatile London apprentices.

The novel as a whole follows the fortunes of those caught up in the Gordon Riots of 1780; Dickens concentrates on the interactions of a small number of Protestant and Catholic families and settles their problems in parallel with the restoration of order by the civic authorities and forces of the Crown. But although the power of the state is reasserted at the end, the authority of parents is seriously undermined. The most authoritarian father figures, Haredale and Willett, are proved wrong and, one way or another, admit their mistakes. It is their houses that are laid waste so spectacularly. The destruction of the physical house in each case allows a greater emphasis on the importance of the dynastic house. The vital principle upheld in the elaboration of family histories in the novel is that of succession, of the effective transferral of responsibility from one generation to the next. Willett as father, and Haredale as uncle, both resign from their dictatorial roles. Chester, however, does not; he renounces his son, sheds all family obligations, and organizes his life around routines of physical gratification in a way that becomes increasingly repugnant. His sexual adventuring in youth subverts the dynastic principle, producing an offspring whose gipsy blood threatens miscegenation as well as illegitimacy; and yet he remains snug in his lodgings in the Middle Temple while *The Maypole* and *The Warren* burn down.

The strategic homelessness that is a necessary stage in the learning process of Haredale and Willett bears no comparison to the desperate vagrancy of the London malcontents who swell the ranks of the rioters. 'Houselessness' is one of Dickens's most compulsive themes, to be found in his writing at every stage of his career, yet he rarely achieves as vivid an evocation of the anxiety and sense of isolation involved as in his descriptions of Rudge senior, wandering the streets of the capital at night as feverishly as Poe's 'Man of the Crowd'. It is a sense of dispossession that activates many of the rioters, rather than any grasp of the religious issues at stake in this moment of anti-Catholic hysteria; Hugh makes this abundantly clear in his spontaneous adaptation of the watchword of the day:

> 'No Popery, brother!', cried the hangman.
> 'No Property, brother!' responded Hugh. (*BR* 359)

Dickens finds more to sympathize with in the alienated condition of this *lumpenproletariat* than in the selfish bigotry of the aristocratic figureheads of Lord George Gordon and Sir John Chester. Nonetheless, his novel clearly proscribes the violent overthrow of order, reserving its most comprehensive disgust for the outlawed figure of Rudge senior, and its most derisive scepticism for the pretensions of groups like the United Bulldogs. Although there are nominally leaders who are variously motivated in their desire to encourage rioting, the mob is repeatedly described as autonomous, spontaneously self-generating, obeying a logic of its own. It is most often referred to as a human sea, as unpredictable and as an uncontrollable as a natural force: 'Assembling and dispersing with equal suddenness, it is as difficult to follow to its various sources as the sea itself; nor does the parallel stop here, for the ocean is not more fickle and uncertain, more terrible when roused, more unreasonable, or more cruel' (*BR* 475). Dickens was unable to improve on this parallel in *A Tale of Two Cities*, where sea imagery dominates in the descriptions of the French revolutionary mob. Despite the range of motives behind the riots, the behaviour of the mob is ultimately inexplicable. Its ebbing and flowing are according to a dynamic of its own; although the disturbances are quelled by putting soldiers in the streets, Dickens's language suggests that it is rather the internal logic of rioting to be self-negating that ends the crisis. The momentum behind the use of sea imagery culminates in a remarkable passage in which the most catastrophic failure of the protest involves a large part of the mob being absorbed into a pool of burning liquid, a sea of fire:

> They lay in heaps all round this fearful pond, husbands and wives, fathers and sons, mothers and daughters, women with children in their arms and babies at their breasts, and drank until they died...From the burning cellars, where they drank out of hats, pails, buckets, tubs, and shoes, some men were drawn, alive, but all alight from head to foot; who, in their unendurable anguish and suffering, making for anything that had the look of water, rolled, hissing, in this hideous lake, and splashed up liquid fire which lapped in all it met with as it ran along the surface, and neither spared the living nor the dead. (*BR* 618)

This horrific scenario, in which the metaphorical deluge becomes literal, catches fire, and escapes into the streets – and even down people's throats – offers a pointed contrast with the comfort and security of the traditional hearth, where fire is safely contained. The haven of warmth in the bar at *The Maypole* provides the most resonant example of fire being used in a controlled way to heat up a variety of liquid refreshments of a more obviously sustaining nature.

The play of natural forces alluded to in Dickens's characterizations of the mob is brought into focus time and again with an insistence on its libidinal energies. The three rabble-rousers, Simon Tappertit, Hugh, and Dennis, are all implicated in the abduction plot, which has been prepared for well in advance by Simon's erotic fantasies about his master's daughter, Dolly, and by Hugh's brazen assault on her. But the tone and point of view of the passage in which the two kidnapped women, Dolly and Emma, try to comfort each other do not insist on any discrepancy between the rioters' attitudes and that of the narrator; or, for that matter, of the reader:

> When, forgetful for a moment of herself, as she was now, she fell on her knees beside her friend, and bent over her, and laid her cheek to hers, and put her arms about her, what mortal eyes could have avoided wandering to the delicate bodice, the streaming hair, the neglected dress, the perfect abandonment and unconsciousness of the blooming little beauty. Who could look on and see her lavish caresses and endearments, and not desire to be in Emma Haredale's place; to be either her or Dolly; either the hugging or the hugged? Not Hugh. Not Dennis. (*BR* 541)

Although the final attribution of this point of view to Hugh and Dennis may allow readers to backtrack, the preceding sentences draw them into a state of complicity with the spectators' voyeurism. The willingness to be aroused is typical of the mob, but the contagious nature of its subversive desires finds a textual equivalent in this implication of the reader. Just as rioters smash property, so writers break down propriety. Dickens is fascinated by precisely that aspect of the mob's activity that he finds most threatening: its breaching of boundaries, physical and psychological. The main targets of its violence are the prisons: by destroying the means by which it would be punished, it removes all limits to its actions. The arbitrary release of prisoners into the community blurs the boundary between the criminal and the law-abiding. But the mob's most terrifying act in prospect is the release of the Bedlamites, whose infiltration of the rest of society would result in a much more radical disturbance of its organizing categories.

The reason that Gabriel Varden is given such a pivotal role in the story is because he is a locksmith: a guardian of thresholds and boundaries, who guarantees security and the preservation of property. The description of Gabriel at work, plying his hammer melodiously, equates the sounds that he produces with the characteristics of the voice of God: 'It was a perfect embodiment of the still small voice' (*BR* 381). This sanctifying of property relations works alongside a deeply phobic reaction to the invasion and abolition of private space. The rioters lead a nomadic existence, drifting, agitating, eating, drinking, and sleeping gregariously. Their indifference to the categories of private and public and to the existence of separate private and public spheres helps to accelerate the transition from attacks on property to a series of direct assaults on the person. In this connection, the most terrifying moment during the riots is when Simon Tappertit casually pulls a bishop's tooth out of his pocket, making it clear that even the final threshold of the outside of the body has not been respected.

The invasion of bodily space is most vividly apparent in the loss of Joe Willett's arm, a far more serious incursion than the ransacking of *The Maypole* that has so traumatized his father John. Willett senior gradually comes to terms with his son's mutilation by repeating the mantra, 'It was took off at the defence of the Salwanners, in America, where the war is.' For the British forces, the American war was another conflict over property, the military campaign an attempt to forestall the loss of British possessions. For Dickens himself, America came to stand for expropriation, for pirated editions of his books, with a corresponding loss of earnings. When he visited it in person in 1842, he found it both disillusioning and physically threatening.

Dickens's account of his round trip, *American Notes for General Circulation* (1842), is dominated by a sense of panic over not being able to control the situations in which he finds himself. America means being subjected to a series of onslaughts that threaten a complete physical and psychological reorganization of the self. The process of transformation begins on the outward journey; an exceptionally rough crossing and the symptoms of seasickness combine to shake everything – physical objects and preconceptions – out of position. When the storm really gets under way, nothing on board is quite what it seems: 'every nook and corner and individual piece of furniture was something else besides what it pretended to be, and was a mere trap and deception and place of secret stowage, whose ostensible purpose was its least useful one' (*AN* 56). But it is not only his surroundings that are subject to this constant metamorphosis; Dickens's descriptions of himself reflect an awareness of the extent to which he is in the process of exchanging one reality for another, and having to adjust his perspective accordingly. He projects this experience of disorientation onto the ship's captain, the exemplar of authority and control:

> After another interval of total unconsciousness, I found he had gone, and recognized another figure in its place. It seemed to wave and fluctuate before me as though I saw it reflected in an unsteady looking-glass; but I knew it for the captain; and such was the cheerful influence of his face, that I tried to smile; yes, even then I tried to smile. I saw by his gestures that he addressed me; but it was a long time before I could make out that he remonstrated against my standing up to my knees in water – as I was; of course I don't know why. I tried to thank him, but couldn't. I could only point to my boots – or wherever I supposed my boots to be – and say in a plaintive voice, 'Cork soles:' at the same time endeavouring, I am told, to sit down in the pool. Finding that I was quite insensible, and for the time a maniac, he humanely conducted me below. (*AN* 65)

Dickens puts his faith in the captain, the epitome of steadiness, but the figure of the captain is not only disconcertingly out of focus; it is also a mirror-image of Dickens's own instability; the captain is not what he appears to be, and neither is Dickens; the idea that this composite being is in control of the situation may be as illusory as the notion that cork soles will save you when the sea comes over the deck. That the danger is not just physical in scope but much more comprehensive is suggested by a comparison between the experience of seasickness and the social unrest explored in *Barnaby Rudge*: 'If I may be allowed to illustrate my state of mind by such an example, I should say that I was exactly in the condition of the elder Mr Willett, after the incursion of the rioters into his bar at Chigwell' (*AN* 64).

Dickens emerges from this experience of constant metamorphosis determined to proceed very differently on dry land; as the coast of America hoves into view he readies himself to engross the scene and reduce it all to order: 'How I remained on deck, staring about me, and how, though I had as many eyes as Argus, I should have had them all wide open, and all employed on new objects – are topics which I will not prolong this chapter to discuss' (*AN* 73). This is an early appearance by Argus in Dickens's writings; the mythological figure alluded to is Argus *panoptes* (all-eyes), Io's bodyguard, who failed to protect her from rape by Zeus, and whose failure was penalized with metamorphosis into the eyes of the peacock's tail. Fated to change shape, Argus nevertheless lent his name, or epithet, to the foundation of a revolutionary new penal system devised by the English philosopher Jeremy Bentham: panopticism. This system revolved around the use of the panopticon, a central control tower providing a vantage point from which the warders could see, theoretically, into every corner of the prison; in these conditions, the individual prisoner would feel completely robbed of privacy. Although he would not, could not, be kept under perpetual supervision, he would never know when he was being watched and when he was not, leaving him in a state of peculiar vulnerability, psychologically prey to an unremitting sense of exposure and surveillance. Dickens approaches the unknown new social environment of America with the desire to control it imaginatively, to keep things in their place and within his conceptual grasp. But his first contact with an American townscape involves a resurgence of the tendency for things to change their shapes, as he notes of the various shop signs in Boston: 'As I walked along, I kept glancing up at these boards, confidently expecting to see a few of them change into something' (*AN* 76). His reaction to this promise of unruliness is to seek for confirmation of panoptical conditions in which the practice of surveillance could operate effectively. He is relieved to find them in place in Worcester, Massachusetts: 'the idea of any inhabitant being able to hide himself from the public gaze, or to have any secrets from the public eye, was not entertainable for a moment' (*AN* 120).

Dickens spends the greater part of his time exploring institutions such as prisons, mental asylums, 'houses of industry', schools, and correctional centres for juvenile offenders. In many ways the most remarkable of these very characteristic visits is to the Asylum for the Blind in Boston. Dickens pauses just before entering its gates in order to register the advantages of vision and celebrate its pleasures but then is almost immediately struck by the social benefits of blindness:

> It is strange to watch the faces of the blind, and see how free they are from all concealment of what is passing in their thoughts; observing which, a man with eyes may blush to contemplate the mask he wears... If the company at a rout, or drawing-room at court, could only for one time be as unconscious of the eyes upon them as blind men and women are, what secrets would come out, and what a worker of hypocrisy this sight, the loss of which we so much pity, would appear to be! (*AN* 81)

Dickens's over-enthusiasm for blindness is motivated by the recognition that the blind are exempt from the conditions of surveillance. Awareness of the glances of others prompts a defensive reaction, produces role playing. The relation of those in control to those under their control is determined by the gaze of power, which the blind are immune to. Dickens yields up his own power as narrator at this point, deferring to a doctor's account of the deaf, blind, and mute Laura Bridgeman. His own point of view migrates constantly between the opposing positions of watchers and watched.

Perhaps the most dismaying aspect of this protean environment, which is constantly resisting the author's attempts to subject it to one kind of discipline or another, is the instability of its language, which deprives Dickens of his most important means of organizing and making sense of what he perceives around him. His first encounter with American English takes the form of a series of misprisions, a comedy of perpetually sliding meanings:

> 'Dinner, if you please,' said I to the waiter.
>
> 'When?' said the waiter.
>
> 'As quick as possible,' said I.
>
> 'Right away?' said the waiter.
>
> After a moment's hesitation, I answered 'No,' at hazard.
>
> '*Not* right away?' cried the waiter, with an amount of surprise that made me start.
>
> I looked at him doubtfully, and returned, 'No; I would rather have it in this private room. I like it very much.'
>
> At this, I really thought the waiter must have gone out of his mind: as I believe he would have done, but for the interposition of another man, who whispered in his ear, 'Directly.'
>
> 'Well! And that's a fact!' said the waiter, looking helplessly at me: 'Right away.' (*AN* 74)

But the real *tour de force* of linguistic anarchy is a passage that explores the manifold shades of meaning that can be given to the word 'fix' in American English. The more meanings the word accumulates, the more unfixed it becomes; the paradoxical instability of the word 'fix' encapsulates the problem Dickens faces of trying to make sense of America, in a journey of unfixing that uproots him from all the conventions of intelligibility he is used to.

The word and the concept he is most concerned with comprise a seminal American preoccupation: liberty. He reserves his most impassioned sarcasm for a vignette on the subject of slavery in the so-called land of the free. After witnessing the division of a family sold into slavery, he observes snarlingly that the 'champion of Life, Liberty, and the Pursuit of Happiness, who had bought them, rode in the same Train' (*AN* 181). For Dickens, Liberty in the United States is primarily experienced as the taking of liberties. The curtailing of personal freedom takes so many forms it becomes part of the texture of everyday life; unspectacular but ubiquitous. One of the most spectacular and bizarre forms it takes is in the universal phenomenon of spitting. Dickens runs a veritable gauntlet of other men's expectorations. This most peculiar version of the invasion of private space is especially prevalent in Washington – the seat of government and the heart of the Union is also the capital of spitting. As a celebrity, Dickens forfeits all hope of privacy the moment he is recognized. But he is also constantly at the mercy of crowds who subject him to an unremitting scrutiny and press themselves upon him simply because he is a foreigner:

> After dinner, we went down to the railroad again, and took our seats in the cars for Washington. Being rather early, those men and boys who happened to have nothing particular to do, and were curious in foreigners, came (according to custom) round the carriage in which I sat; let down all the windows; thrust in their heads and shoulders; hooked themselves on conveniently, by their elbows; and fell to comparing notes on the subject of my personal appearance, with as much indifference as if I were a stuffed figure. I never gained so much uncompromising information with reference to my own nose and eyes, the various impressions wrought by my mouth and chin on different minds, and how my head looks when it is viewed behind, as on these occasions. Some gentlemen were only satisfied by exercising their sense of touch; and the boys (who are surprisingly precocious in America) were seldom satisfied, even by that, but would return to the charge over and over again. Many a budding president has walked into my room with his cap on his head and his hands in his pockets, and stared at me for two whole hours: occasionally refreshing himself with a tweak of his nose, or a draught from the water-jug; or by walking to the windows and inviting other boys in the street below, to come up and do likewise:

> crying, 'Here he is!' 'Come on!' 'Bring all your brothers!' with other hospitable entreaties of that nature. (*AN* 162)

The would-be surveillance operative is made a total spectacle of. The tone is amused rather than indignant, but there is no doubting the sense of discomfort as verbal anatomizing gives way to practical investigation; no tooth or arm is at stake, but the failure to observe boundaries is disturbing in ways that relate distantly to the outrages of *Barnaby Rudge*. Except that, in America, the freedom to take liberties is intrinsic to the culture; the intrusive boy is a budding president, rather than an embryonic outlaw; but the problem of America is that he is just as likely to become the one as the other.

Dickens's itinerary takes him through a number of states, and a variety of urban and rural settings, but the two most defining moments of his trip occur in places that seem utterly remote from each other in every conceivable way until they become joined in Dickens's imagination. One is the cell occupied by the prisoner in solitary confinement, in the Eastern Penitentiary in Pennsylvania; the other is the open prairie at the furthest point in Dickens's westward journey, before he turns round to return to the eastern seaboard. The conditions inside the Eastern Penitentiary share many features with the panoptical system, which Dickens shows considerable enthusiasm for when he first encounters it in Boston. But the main emphasis in Philadelphia is on physical and psychological isolation of an intensity that Dickens is unprepared for:

> Standing at the central point, and looking down these dreary passages, the dull repose and quiet that prevails, is awful. Occasionally, there is a drowsy sound from some lone weaver's shuttle, or shoemaker's last, but it is stifled by the thick walls and heavy dungeon-door, and only serves to make the general stillness more profound. Over the head and face of every prisoner who comes into this melancholy house, a black hood is drawn; and in this dark shroud, an emblem of the curtain dropped between him and the living world, he is led to the cell from which he never again comes forth, until his whole term of imprisonment has expired. He never hears of wife or children; home or friends; the life or death of any single creature. He sees the prison-officers, but with that exception he never looks upon a human countenance, or hears a human voice. He is a man buried alive; to be dug out in the slow round of years;

> and in the mean time dead to everything but torturing anxieties and horrible despair. (*AN* 148)

Remarkably, Dickens was to reuse many of the details of this description in his account of Dr Manette's incarceration in the Bastille, in *A Tale of Two Cities*. He makes a particular feature of the shoemaker's last, and turns the concept of burial alive into an organizing strategy in the later text. The penal system of the revolutionary culture of the United States is shown to be no more progressive than the *Ancien Régime* seen in its worst light. It is not just the prisoner's liberty that is confiscated, but his entire private life, the very means with which to construct a sense of self. Long-term imprisonment on these terms results in degeneration of the senses, an approach towards the total sensory deprivation of a Laura Bridgeman. But, whereas Laura Bridgeman is drawn slowly out of her isolation, the prisoner in Philadelphia is driven further and further inside his.

This appalling loss of liberty might be contrasted with the prospect held out by the prairie, which is on such an enormous scale, and which is defined by its sense of limitlessness, by the complete absence of any boundaries. But Dickens's reaction to its vast emptiness is surprisingly claustrophobic:

> It would be difficult to say why, or how – though it was possibly from having heard and read so much about it – but the effect on me was disappointment. Looking towards the setting sun, there lay, stretched out before my view, a vast expanse of level ground; unbroken, save by one thin line of trees, which scarcely amounted to a scratch upon the great blank; until it met the glowing sky, wherein it seemed to dip: mingling with its rich colours, and mellowing in its distant blue. There it lay, a tranquil sea or lake without water, if such a simile be admissible, with the day going down upon it: a few birds wheeling here and there: and solitude and silence reigning paramount around. But the grass was not yet high; there were bare black patches on the ground; and the few wild flowers that the eye could see, were poor and scanty. Great as the picture was, its very flatness and extent, which left nothing to the imagination, tamed it down and cramped its interest. I felt little of that sense of freedom and exhilaration which a Scottish heath inspires, or even our English downs awaken. It was lonely and wild, but oppressive in its barren monotony. I felt that in traversing the Prairies, I could never abandon myself to the scene, forgetful of all else; as I should do instinctively, were the heather underneath my feet, or an iron-bound

> coast beyond; but should often glance towards the distant and frequently-receding line of the horizon, and wish it gained and passed. It is not a scene to be forgotten, but it is scarcely one, I think (at all events, as I saw it), to remember with much pleasure, or to covet the looking-on again, in after life. (*AN* 226)

Solitude; silence; a feeling of being cramped; no sense of freedom: these are the conditions of the Penitentiary. Whether he is contemplating the innermost cell in a prison, or the widest of the West's wide open spaces, what Dickens finds in America is something fundamentally inhibiting and alienating. It is also what he finds in himself; the particular stretch of Prairie he chooses to experience is called the Looking-Glass Prairie, a name that recalls his encounter with the looking-glass figure of the Captain on board ship. America reflects back all of Dickens's anxieties about the management of thresholds: between public and private; power and powerlessness; discipline and a loss of control.

It is the failure of language to provide a means of stabilizing the relations between these sets of alternatives that Dickens identifies as radically undermining. In *Martin Chuzzlewit* (1843–4), the chapters that deal with Martin's attempts to establish an architectural practice in America focus on the linguistic treacheries of American English. Martin's first encounter with Americans is with newspapermen, with their deliberately systematic misrepresentations, their overwhelming concentration on slander, their utter and complete invasion of privacy, and their omnipresence. The newspapers of New York do not inform their public so much as perform a series of assaults on them; as the list of newspaper names makes clear, America represents itself to itself as a society organized by intimidation, as a notional democracy regulated by force much more than by consent:

> 'Here's this morning's New York Sewer!' cried one. 'Here's this morning's New York Stabber! Here's the New York Family Spy! Here's the New York Private Listener! Here's the New York Peeper! Here's the New York Plunderer! Here's the New York Keyhole Reporter! Here's the New York Rowdy Journal! Here's all the New York papers!' (*MC* 249)

This is the vocabulary of rioting and of surveillance combined; transferred from the streets and buildings, from both public and private spaces, to become the medium of thought and perception, typifying the way Americans conduct their relations with a series of psychic violations. In anticipation of tabloid journalism, what is most secret becomes most exposed, what is most newsworthy is what is least worthy of attention. Martin is astonished to discover his private correspondence is being published in the *Watertoast Gazette*, including his polite refusals of begging requests, his declining invitations to public engagements; he himself becomes an object for representation, his body written up exhaustively, with a thoroughness that subtracts rather than adds meaning to the representation:

> Two gentlemen connected with the Watertoast Gazette had come express to get the matter for an article on Martin. They had agreed to divide the labour. One of them took below the waistcoat; one above. Each stood directly in front of his subject with his head a little on one side, intent on his department. If Martin put one boot before the other, the lower gentlemen was down upon him; he rubbed a pimple on his nose, and the upper gentleman booked it. He opened his mouth to speak, and the same gentleman was on one knee before him, looking in at his teeth, with the nice scrutiny of a dentist. (*MC* 350)

This last detail, with its repetition of the oral threat found elsewhere, puts a slightly different complexion on the otherwise amusing pantomime. The division of labour admits failure in advance for any project that aims to capture the personality, matching the details of external appearance to a knowledge of character. Unsurprisingly, 'amateurs in the physiognomical and phrenological sciences' are at hand, roving in Martin's vicinity 'with watchful eyes and itching fingers, and sometimes one, more daring than the rest, made a mad grasp at the back of his head and vanished in the crowd' (*MC* 350). These desperate acts of interpretation, which lead to nothing, are more than usually futile in a society where surface *always* belies reality; in which protests against slavery cover racial hatred, while condemnation of the class structure is an alibi for phenomenal snobbery, and reports of urban development refer to an area of fetid swamp. It is the land agent who sells a part of 'Eden' to Martin and Mark Tapley who sums up this culture of deceit:

> Two gray eyes lurked deep within this agent's head, but one of them had no sight in it, and stood stock still. With that side of his face he seemed to listen to what the other side was doing. Thus each profile had a distinct expression; and when the moveable side was most in action, the rigid one was in its coldest state of watchfulness. It was like turning the man inside out, to pass to that view of his features in his liveliest mood, and see how calculating and intent they were. (*MC* 338)

Here the division of labour takes place within the same individual, who performs the act of inspection on himself. He embodies a system of control predicated on the destruction of privacy, by a form of psychological dispossession, by insisting on its right to turn all its citizens inside out.

In *Hard Times* (1854), it is the language of British culture that is anatomized, with the usage both of those in authority and of their political opponents being condemned for its dislocations, its lack of congruence with the lives of the inhabitants of Coketown. Mr Gradgrind's utilitarian approach to language implants value only in those words that have reference to facts, even, or especially, when such facts are abstractions from the sensual reality of the speaker's experience. Bitzer's famous definition of a horse ('Quadruped. Graminivorous. Forty teeth...' etc. (*HT* 12)) has a merely taxonomic accuracy that does not allow him to express the meaning that horses may have had, or might have, in the sphere of everyday life. In Dotheboys Hall, the relation between taxonomic definition and everyday life is enforced as the most direct means of asserting authority. In Coketown, the act of divorcing taxonomy from everyday life is the measure of power exerted by those in authority over the powerless, whose experience contradicts the priorities of the taxonomic order.

Rebellion is organized against that order, but it is expressed in the political oratory of Slackbridge, whose formulaic repetitions ('Oh my friends and fellow-sufferers, and fellow-workmen, and fellow-men!' (*HT* 141)) draw attention to its separation from experience, as Stephen Blackpool quietly points out in his address to the crowd: '"My brothers," said Stephen, whose low voice was distinctly heard, "and my fellow-workmen – for that yo are to me, though not, as I knows on, to this delegate heer...''' (*HT* 145). Both authority and rebellion are objects of mistrust in *Hard Times*, their political motivations in either case prohibiting the use of the individual imagination, and proscribing, scapegoating even, those who have the imagination to remain individual. Sissy Jupe, who knows more about horses than anyone else in the class, is reduced to silence by the systematic redefinition of everything she knows at first-hand, including her own name, and the occupation of her father, until everything that constitutes her as an individual has been replaced by conformity to the taxonomic order, and she herself has become 'girl number twenty'. Stephen Blackpool is the point of resistance to political conformity, which is expressed in a language of 'wind', whether this is blowing from the direction of Slackbridge in the chapter entitled 'Men and Brothers', or from Bounderby in the chapter entitled 'Men and Masters'. His own language is grounded in the priorities of direct personal communication; Dickens places more value in his private compact with one other individual than in the illusion of cooperation represented by the 'United Aggregate Tribunal'. Stephen's expulsion from the community together with his final redemption provide a focus on the linguistic intimidations of British culture, whose most valuable resource, sincerity, is in danger of being lost, of perishing through neglect. It is the difficult relation between sincerity and public address, confidentiality and mass communication, that Dickens tries to come to terms with in the more complex articulations of his fiction in the first person.

4

First Person

DAVID COPPERFIELD, URANIA COTTAGE

It is not unusual that in novels with a strong autobiographical bias even though a fictional one, the process of self-examination should include a watchfulness over the visible image of the self that is presented to others. It is hardly surprising, therefore, that the text of *David Copperfield* (1850) should be occasionally punctuated by moments in which David carefully considers his own image in a mirror. But it is intriguing that he should choose to do so at moments of heightened anxiety and distress, when he pores over the reflection of his external appearance with a morbid fascination at just those moments when his desire to be alone, one would think, ought to be construed as a desire to hide his sufferings, to conceal them from view. One such occasion is when he has been banished to his room after a beating by the odious Murdstone: 'I crawled up from the floor, and saw my face in the glass, so swollen, red and ugly that it almost frightened me. My stripes were sore and stiff, and made me cry afresh, when I moved; but they were nothing to the guilt I felt' (*DC* 62). The process of contemplating the image of the beaten and punished self is what actually contributes to the production of guilt. Even more striking and peculiar is the force of this compulsion to look in the mirror that overcomes David even after the occasion of his mother's death: 'I stood upon a chair when I was left alone, and looked into the glass to see how red my eyes were, and how sorrowful my face' (*DC* 123). It is this curiosity about the self that others might see that provides a vivid introduction to the chronic division in David's sense of self that the novel as a whole elaborates.

Parallel to David's inspection of his own face within the frame of a mirror is his espial of other faces similarly framed by appearing in windows, and it is clear enough that on such occasions what David is seeing in these faces are projections of his own sense of self. The most obvious case arises when David pays a visit to his old childhood home at Blunderstone. The house has recently been reoccupied, after a period of being empty, by no less than a 'poor lunatic gentleman' who is actually stationed in David's own old room, 'sitting at my little window, looking out into the churchyard; and I wondered whether his rambling thoughts ever went upon any of the fancies that used to occupy mine' (*DC* 300). David no longer has any kin in that house, but the possibility of a kinship of state of mind is tentatively suggested in this daydream about shared 'fancies'.

The lunatic is not the only face at a window belonging to someone prone to fancies whose description might also be a projection of David himself. When David has lost both his parents and all means of support, when he has been stripped of everything that had composed his former identity, and stripped even of most of his clothes, he arrives at the house of his aunt Betsey. The first thing to confront him there is a face in the window, that of Mr Dick. Both David and Dick are engaged in writing 'memorials', but, whereas David has to settle his account and come to a conclusion, has to present a definitive biographical portrait of himself, Mr Dick is engaged on a task that will never come to an end: 'for if anything were certain under the sun, it was certain that the Memorial never would be finished' (*DC* 207). David often speaks using the manner of the professional novelist that Dickens was, clearly aware of an audience he has to cater for, despite his occasional professions to the effect that 'this manuscript is intended for no eyes but mine' (*DC* 559). He indicates at various points that he feels under the pressure of satisfying expectations, of producing copy, of not 'meandering', of getting on with the job, of being a professional; in short, he frequently conducts himself as if he were subject to the same constraints of nineteenth-century serial publication and distribution as his author. Mr Dick is blissfully unconcerned with these practicalities; his method of distribution is by kite: 'I don't know where they may come down. It's according to circumstances, and the wind, and so forth; but I take my chance of that' (*DC* 195). Such nonchalance would be an enviable alternative not just to David's programme of tasks, but to Dickens's as well; the name Dick is, of course, an abbreviated form of Dickens.

Dick also enjoys another advantage besides that of distribution by kite: the advantage of being mad, of being able to indulge his fancies while at the same time being taken seriously. According to Aunt Betsey, his advice is sounder than anyone else's, and he has an oracular authority for her. He also enjoys the advantage of being a child, of not being a real subject of autobiography; not having to grow up to be the subject of a process of growth and maturing and of the acquiring of self-knowledge. The subjectivity of Dick is something that stops still or goes into reverse; he is at his happiest with childish pursuits and when he is accepted as a playfellow by David's contemporaries at Dr Strong's school. He also enjoys the advantage of adoption; he and David are both adopted, in a novel whose world, like that of *The Pickwick Papers*, makes a disaster area of natural families. There are hardly any complete families in *David Copperfield* (the Micawbers are a dubious exception) and the catastrophes wreaked by natural families can be repaired only by judicious adopting.

In a sense, the figure of the 'poor lunatic' at Blunderstone represents what happens if you do not get adopted – if you get left behind. It is almost a representation of what David might have become if he had remained in the context of his original family home, part of a natural family as opposed to an adoptive one: incarcerated, confined, a gloomy melancholic. Whereas, Dick's way of life is much more carefree and even occasionally uplifted in its delusions (as his kite-flying suggests). Dick has none of the responsibilities that destroy families in the novel, he is utterly unworldly; the only money he has he keeps in his pocket for the pleasure of rattling, not to spend.

Of course, these alternative projections of David do not in any sense represent a desire on his part to identify with any particular image or representation of another way of life. The differences between them start to show that what the text is constructed to do is to keep the image of its narrator an imprecise and even volatile one. The other figure that David becomes increasingly identified with, in terms of a mania for verbal elaboration, and for *writing*, is of course that of Mr Micawber. Micawber's letters interspersed throughout the body of David's narrative achieve, more than the productions of anyone else, almost the status of separate texts. (Once you have read the whole novel, you have also read a small Micawber œuvre.) Even when Micawber is able to deliver a spoken message in person, he prefers to resort to written testimony, as at the climactic moment when he exposes Uriah Heep: he simply reads out to the assembled company his own letter of discovery and denunciation. It is Micawber's brand of evasive bravado – a use of language that provides him with a kind of self-advertising camouflage – that David notes he himself is equally prone to. During the critical stage of his engagement to Dora, David mentally registers the fact that his despairing letter to Dora's confidante, Miss Mills, is 'something in the style of Mr Micawber'. Micawber's habitual manner is only intensified during the period when he has to conceal his personal motivations in order to be able to lay successfully a trap for Heep; but the characterization of his behaviour that is given at this point could stand as a description of the procedure adopted by the narrator of the novel: vacillating 'between an evident disposition to reveal something, and a counter-disposition to reveal nothing' (*DC* 653).

For David – for the narrator – identifications are momentary and provisional, part of a process marked by a series of restless substitutions; many of David's projections of himself are in effect needed to evacuate certain aspects of his personality rather than fill them in. On occasion, he seems concerned not so much to build up a picture of himself as to take several successive opportunities to consign parts of himself to oblivion, as when he puts himself in the place of his dead younger half-brother: 'The mother who lay in the grave, was the mother of my infancy; the little creature in her arms, was myself, as I had once been, hushed for ever on her bosom' (*DC* 131). Later, when David becomes head boy at Dr Strong's school, he looks back on his former self as a newcomer 'as something I have passed, rather than have actually been – and almost think of him as someone else' (*DC* 254). At the critical point when he is haunted by anxiety over Agnes but is about to become infatuated with Dora, he goes alone to see a play tellingly entitled *The Stranger*, and is inexplicably 'so dreadfully cut up' by the experience that 'I hardly knew myself in my own glass when I got home' (*DC* 359). Here the problematical relationship between external appearance and emotional reality reaches an extreme point of alienation.

That sense of provisionality that hovers around David's identity during his childhood and adolescence is felt as both unwelcome and threatening, and would have been the outcome of his not being in control of his own life, of not being able to create his own opportunities; it goes with a feeling of being forced into a variety of strange and unsettling roles – a species of imposition suggested by the variety of names given to him in the course of his early life. Christened David Copperfield, the protagonist is also expected to answer to the name of Murdstone, and is subsequently obliged to accept the addition of Trotwood, not to mention the use of nicknames: Brooks of Sheffield, Doady, and the most ambiguous of all, which is Steerforth's favourite name for him, Daisy. (The initial letters of David's Christian name and surname compose an inversion of Dickens's own names, a fact that the writer professed amazement at when it was first pointed out to him by his son-in-law and first biographer, John Forster.)

It is not only proper nouns but also pronouns that are occasionally knocked out of true in this text – especially the first-person pronoun in this autobiographical account. The first person crops up sometimes when it is grammatically incongruent, or when the awkwardness of the phrasing deployed around it gives it an unsettled and unsettling quality. David's account of his earliest attempts at walking includes the following sentence: 'I believe I can remember these two [his mother and Peggotty] at a little distance apart, dwarfed to my sight by stooping down or kneeling on the floor, and I going unsteadily from the one to the other'(*DC* 21). The reader is not given quite what is expected here. Instead of 'I' we might expect to see 'myself': I believe I can remember these two – and I believe I can remember myself going unsteadily... The grammar stumbles a little, and in doing so it gives added definition to the image presented here of faltering steps; it helps to underline the fact that the 'I' in this text – the sense of self that attaches to the use of the first-person singular pronoun – does indeed go very unsteadily.

The notion of a provisionality of sense of self is both potentially liberating and threatening at one and the same time. Even Mr Dick, who appears to have been released from the imprisonment of his former life into a world of fancies, provides an awareness of the degree of risk involved in consigning a part of oneself – a part of one's life – to oblivion. Dick is constantly assailed by the compulsion to figure the great moment of crisis in his life in terms of the beheading of Charles I; the decisive moment is supposed to have involved all the troubles in King Charles's mind being taken out and put into Mr Dick's head. The image of a beheading stands for the severing of any psychological connections, any conscious memories of his former life, that Dick might otherwise retain. The beheading is what prevents him from finishing his 'Memorial' because he finds it impossible to eradicate all mention of it from the composition of his manuscripts. On the other hand, Dick's fiction about the beheading is precisely what he needs in order to prevent the realizing of those crucial psychological connections, and so he has to keep it going; the writing of the 'Memorial' becomes the means of preventing him from doing any genuine, and therefore dangerous, remembering. Revealingly, Dickens's own account of the death of Charles I, in his *A Child's History of England*, stresses the very last word the king is supposed to have uttered: 'Remember!' The extraordinary tension that builds up behind the ratio of remembering to forgetting is focused on Dick, but it also surfaces at the heart of other situations in the plot. Wickfield diagnoses his own condition in parallel terms: 'Weak indulgence has ruined me. Indulgence in remembrance, and indulgence in forgetfulness' (*DC* 534). The situation that is most chronically affected by the pressure of needing to get the balance right is, of course, that of the autobiographical narrator himself.

David also ponders the threat of beheading, the question of the connection or disconnection of the head from the body, as a means of testing imaginatively whether any given experience is to be considered a genuine or integral part of the life that he is narrating. He refers, for example, to the problem of the relationship of Heep and Agnes as having become 'a part of my life, and as inseparable from my life as my own head'

(*DC* 359). It is impossible to ignore the extremely violent implications of the decapitation of Charles I and it is worth considering what basis for comparison there might be between the images of beheading in the text and other frequent images of mutilation to human bodies or of signs of damage having been done to them at some critical juncture in their past. What is particularly striking is that the most arresting signs of violent damage, or threats of violence, are to be found on the bodies of women or directed at women. One of the most obvious cases is that of Miss Dartle, who has suffered something related to decapitation: a blow to the face with a hammer, which has left her with a scar that functions as the most expressive part of her body; her whole being is organized around it, and it divides her life into two. Her existence subsequent to that traumatic event has formed into a process of sharpening that has turned her, almost as an embodiment of retaliation, into an offensive weapon, so that she is 'all edge'. And she herself acts as a kind of relay for the type of violence once inflicted on her, expressing her willingness, her desire even, to see Emily whipped and to have her branded on the face, after the elopement with Steerforth – the very character responsible for striking Miss Dartle with the hammer in the first place.

The action of striking a woman and marking her comes to seem almost definitive of the condition of womanhood in this text. Apart from the attention that is drawn to specific named characters in the book, there is also the great generic incident on the road to Dover, which has an almost archetypal quality for David as he looks back, regarding the scene as unforgettable. This is when the tinker woman is knocked down by her partner. The relevant passage gives the incident an unusual, although unexplained significance:

> I never shall forget seeing her fall backward on the hard road, and lie there with her bonnet tumbled off, and hair all whitened in the dust; nor, when I looked back from a distance, seeing her sitting on the pathway, which was a bank by the roadside, wiping the blood from her face with a corner of her shawl, while he went on ahead. (*DC* 181)

The passage has great resonance, first because it is obviously meant to be conveying something fundamental about the particular relationship in question; secondly, because it recalls so many other instances of assaulted women, described or alluded to. Even David's own timid and powerless mother is capable of expressing the alternative to being married to Murdstone in terms that make the choice one between physical and psychological oppression, each of which clearly reflects on the other: 'Would you wish me to shave my head and black my face, or disfigure myself with a burn, or a scald, or something of that sort?' (*DC* 28). And Peggotty, who is being addressed at this point, and who seems equally remote from the threat of violence, almost impregnable in the degree of comfort she seems to exude, curiously attracts to herself a variety of figurative and literal sharp points or edges that puncture her skin or impinge on it: her dark eyes 'seemed to darken their whole neighbourhood in her face, and [her] cheeks and arms [were] so hard and red that I wondered the birds didn't peck her in preference to the apples' (*DC* 21). On another occasion, when the young David is reading to Peggotty out of his 'Crocodile' book, he notices that she is 'thoughtfully sticking her needle into various parts of her face and arms, all the time' (*DC* 26). Peggotty actually bears the same Christian name as David's mother, Clara, which helps to run together even more easily the figures of these two different women.

There is another kind of association between the damage offered to women and the circumstance of Charles I's beheading and the significance it has for Mr Dick. One of the things the beheading does come to mean for Dick is a loss of manhood; after the beheading as Dick conceives of it, he becomes a child again, a stranger to adult sexuality. And if he ceases to be a man in this sense, then there is a possibility that what he becomes instead is somewhat closer to the condition of a woman, in a text where women are repeatedly defined in relation to wounds, cuts, piercings, scars, and other analogues of beheading. And this is important in view of the fact that the most frequently posited alternative identity for David is not that of a lunatic or of a child, but of a woman: the identity of Betsey Trotwood Copperfield, the girl that David might have become, the girl who at the moment of his birth became as it were suspended 'for ever in the land of dreams and shadows' (*DC* 20). But suspended over David is what she definitely remains; she has a very real presence in the mind of Aunt Betsey, who wanted to adopt a girl child, but who adopts David instead after a lapse of many years, only to keep on insisting on the way that the sister would have grown up, and behaved, and thought, and felt: quite differently from the way that David has turned out: 'He has run away' she observes of David when he turns up in Dover, "Ah! His sister, Betsey Trotwood, never would have run away." My aunt shook her head firmly, confident in the character and behaviour of the girl who never was born' (*DC* 186). When Aunt Betsey asks for David's opinion of Mr Dick, she challenges him, 'Come! Your sister Betsey Trotwood would have told me what she thought of anyone, directly. Be as like your sister as you can, and speak out!' (*DC* 195). And there is this much that binds together the identities of Mr Dick, David and David's imaginary sister, that, whereas David has in a sense supplanted his own sister, Dick has also been filling the role of substitute for her; as Aunt Betsey advises David, she has 'had the benefit of his society and advice for these last ten years and upwards – in fact, ever since your sister, Betsey Trotwood, disappointed' (*DC* 195–6). Perhaps even more disconcertingly – because it comes from a complete stranger – almost the first thing that Steerforth ever says to David makes it clear that he detects in him a certain amount of femininity, regards him in the light of the potential girl he has only very narrowly failed to become:

> 'You haven't got a sister, have you?' said Steerforth, yawning.
>
> 'No,' I answered.
>
> 'That's a pity,' said Steerforth. 'If you had had one, I should think she would have been a pretty, timid, little, bright-eyed sort of girl. I should have liked to know her.' (*DC* 90)

The writing in this novel is experimenting constantly with the idea that, if David is to be given an alternative identity; if his social, familial, and sexual identities are made fluid, provisional, slightly nomadic in character, then the nearest alternative that could be offered to him is that of a woman, or of a girl; of the sister and daughter that were in contention with the son and brother he actually became. But at one level of the text, son and brother is what he is constantly in danger of *un*becoming. And the process involved here would resemble decapitation, would be a form of mutilation, or castration. It is not for nothing that the young David is fascinated, whenever he visits Peggotty's house, by two books: one is Foxe's *Book of Martyrs*, the other is the 'Crocodile book', which becomes one of the most constant factors of his entire life from earliest childhood to married adulthood. The torments suffered by the Protestant martyrs speak for themselves; while the crocodile is a very type for children of potential physical violence (it is the figure in the Punch and Judy show that wolfs down the sausages). According to the narrator's information, the only way to deal with a crocodile is to put sharp pieces of timber down its throat, a savage remedy that echoes Peggotty sticking needles into her face and Rosa Dartle being struck across the face with a hammer. The first thing that ever happens to David in the book is very close to decapitation, because we are told that he is born with a caul and that he is subsequently made very uneasy when he has to part with it, when it is sold: 'I remember to have felt quite uncomfortable and confused, at a part of myself being disposed of in that way' (*DC* 12).

What is unusual about this first-person narrative is that in many ways it goes completely against the grain of conventional biographical form, orientated towards *Bildung*, the building or formation of character; in the face of the expected autobiographical inquisition, the self-scrutiny that is geared to a steady consolidation of identity, the accumulation of knowledge, the measuring of growth, the registering of development, what the text provides instead is a form of writing that almost throws that process into reverse; to adapt one of Peggotty's formulations, instead of approaching a sense of self that emerges from the chronological layering of a sequential account, what the reader gets is almost the opposite, not a proper first person, not a proper 'I', at all. Instead, as Peggotty says – as she screams rather – : 'Here's my Am! Growed out of knowledge' (*DC* 36). Of course, the book goes through the motions of constructing a civic self, and in fact it can be quite legalistic about it; it goes through an elaborate pantomime of providing its narrator with a watertight alibi, with a legally unimpeachable account of events, derived from the evidence of 'credible witnesses' whose reports are scrupulously recorded as being 'in part confirmed by' others, and so on; there is an extensive employment of legal vocabulary, and it often seems as if the narrator is concerned to draw up proof, to prepare his defence, going more than halfway to meet the expectation of a document that will secure for the reader a proper awareness of David's civic identity, his social position and formal relations with others. It is exactly the correct register to employ for one who has been trained to be a Proctor in Doctor's Commons, in a world in which a majority of the main male characters are concerned more or less directly with legal proceedings: Traddles, Wickfield, Spenlow, Heep, Dick, Micawber, to name only those who are at some stage or another actually employed in a legal capacity; all of them apart from Traddles – the exception who proves the rule – nurturing a hidden life that escapes representation in their legal dealings. Indeed, it seems that the clarification of identity required by legal institutions often produces its opposite; so that even Spenlow, for example, proves to have evaded what one would consider absolutely inevitable for a lawyer, when it is discovered after his death that he has failed to make a will. This is perhaps because he is acutely aware of what happens in a registration process that does not result in taxonomy and the preservation of records but in confusion and dereliction.

The legal register is employed extensively but it is frequently made irrelevant, rendered inadequate, by the irresistible pull the writing feels towards images of lunacy, towards the company of half-wits, towards flights of fancy, towards repeated demonstrations, in the behaviour of Mr Dick, of the need for a complete redefinition of the meanings of common sense, perception, insight, and even of counsel, since Dick acts as the delightfully parodic version of a legal adviser to Aunt Betsey. (Later on, of course, he is actually employed in copying legal documents that are constantly threatened with interference by the *idée fixe* of Charles I.) Similarly, although the book traces the advance in years of its central character and mimics the tracing-out of a process of growth and maturing, at the same time it constantly reverts to images of childhood not only in a retrospective review of David's own life, but in the recognition of childish states of mind and feelings in those who are chronologically adult. And, beyond that, it processes a great deal of material that puts considerable obstacles in the way of the construction of a straightforwardly male sexual identity for its narrator; it is quite radically divided in this respect perhaps more than in any other.

But, in spite of its interest in the illegitimate, the irrational, and the irresponsible, which is what in terms of Victorian ideology the writing shows a tendency to be organized around, it is also haunted, almost literally, by the priorities of an authoritarian and paternalistic order. When David is born, posthumously, the doctor who delivers him is said to walk like the ghost in *Hamlet*: the ghost, in other words, of someone's father. David's obsession with his own father's grave is particularly stimulated by his concern, once he has heard the story of Lazarus, that the dead are 'all lying in their graves at rest' (*DC* 22), and that his father has not risen to haunt him. References to *Hamlet* are sustained throughout the text and compounded in their effect by the support of references to *Macbeth*, particularly in connection with the appearance of Banquo's ghost at the feast. For Macbeth, it is the appearance or disappearance of the ghost that determines the very possibility of being a man, which is to say, being manly. Steerforth actually quotes the relevant line: 'Why, [the ghost] being gone, I am a man again' (*DC* 302). Banquo, of course, as ancestor to a line of kings, is a distinctly patriarchal figure. The text is shadowed by these intimations of a vengeful paterfamilias, warning the errant protagonist back onto the straight and narrow path; but, although the authority of the Shakespearean references and the awe in which David quite naturally holds his father's grave suggest a latent power, this power is also quite precisely depleted by its pastness, by its residual function. It is no less but also no more than a ghostly presence.

By far the most sustained and concerted campaign that the text mounts against the claims of conventional biographical form consists in its attempts to disperse all social, sexual, legal, and rational definitions and delimitations in the oblivion of drowning. When David is deprived of his caul, his caul is available to be sold, and the expectation is that it will be sold to sailors, because the popular superstition is that a caul acts as a preventative against drowning. Once he has lost his caul, David can drown. And that is precisely what he tries to do metaphorically, and what very many of the other characters do literally, all the way through the text. Steerforth drowns; before he does, he is called a 'nautical phenomenon', and Mr Peggotty misnames him revealingly as 'Rudderford', suggesting that there is something in his personality that is steering him inexorably in the direction of drowning. After his death, his bereaved mother and Rosa Dartle are pictured staring into space, in a manner that 'made it seem as if the gathering waters would encompass them' (*DC* 621). Little Em'ly does not actually drown, but her ruin is anticipated by her 'springing forward to her destruction, directed far out to sea'; 'would it have been better', wonders David, 'for little Em'ly to have had the waters close above her head that morning in my sight' (*DC* 43). Ham is drowned. Both Emily and Ham are the orphans of fathers who were drowned and David queries whether Ham was not christened the way he was because the Peggotty house is like a Noah's Ark, the boat that was built to survive the flood in which nearly everyone was drowned. Jack Maldon, whose fortunes are decided for him, describes his personal passage to India as a 'plunge into water'; Wickfield's descent into senility and depression is a process he says of being 'drowned'. David dreams, after meeting Uriah Heep, of the latter launching Peggotty's house/boat on a 'piratical expedition', 'carrying me and little Em'ly to the Spanish Main, to be drowned' (*DC* 225). His infatuation with Dora is described as a sensation of being emotionally waterlogged: 'Enough love might have been wrung out of me, metaphorically speaking, to drown anybody in' (*DC* 439). Paradoxically, he regards Dora herself as a means of rescue from this plight: 'Dora, who was the stay and anchor of my tempest-driven bark' (*DC* 504). Mr Peggotty swears that he is ready to drown as long as there is a man he can trust remaining to look after Emily; then, he says, 'I could go down quieter'. Finally, Barkis dies in his bed, but he gives up the ghost at the exact moment that the tide goes out.

The writing is in any case irresistibly drawn towards the sea and to the Yarmouth setting where the land and sea are mixed up, the 'town' and the 'tide' being given equal weight, the town in fact living according to the rhythms of the tide. Mr Peggotty's house built out of a boat is the most prominent visual reminder of this amphibian existence. But even when the writing takes the reader well inland imaginatively, the temptation to give descriptions a marine undertow is often yielded to. At Blunderstone Rookery, the old rooks' nests burdening the higher branches of the elm trees swing 'like wrecks upon a stormy sea' (*DC* 15). In this respect, David's most significant *alter ego*, aside from that of Betsey Trotwood Copperfield, is the one that Quinion gives him: Davey Jones – the David against whom a caul is no proof, the David whose locker means the dissolving of all attempts to construct identity, the undoing of all patient demonstration, the disintegration of everything composed.

The refuges of lunacy, childishness, and female personae can be seen as desperate expedients in the attempt to escape conformity to a given role, expedients whose cost is counted as perhaps too high and for which the only alternative appears to be the negative escape of watery extinction, of dissolution; the neutralizing tactic of anaesthesia, loss of consciousness. What David sees in the sea is precisely nothing: a loss of the focus his task as memorialist requires him to train on his situation. At one point, he actually looks at the sea through a telescope that should sharpen distinctions, make things even uncomfortably clear, but mercifully 'I could make out nothing myself when it was put to my eye, but I pretended I could' (*DC* 31); this in a chapter entitled 'I Observe'. The only one of the creatures of David's imagination who survives that long looked-for embrace with the nothingness of the sea survives it precisely because his subsequent existence is on a desert island where no one will ever see him and judge the degree of his conformism or nonconformism. But David's fantasy about Robinson Crusoe leaves out of account the eventual companionship of Friday. What he stresses instead is Crusoe's solitude, the fact that he is better off than David himself precisely because no one is looking at him; Crusoe 'had nobody to look at him and see that he was solitary' (*DC* 75). The emphasis on external appearance and the extent to which it matches a sense of identity is pursued by many of Dickens's characters; the insecurity over this relationship, which arises when it is tested and challenged by the gaze of others, also reflects back on the situation of the writer himself. What the figure of Crusoe escapes is the fate of the professional novelist who has to court attention in order to survive; of the monthly or weekly serialist for whom the risk of exposure to vulgar scrutiny brings as many anxieties as rewards, for whom the sense of being under the public gaze is powerfully intensified. The measure of suffering, even, that this could induce is evoked by that episode in the schoolyard of David's youth, when he is forced to wander with a placard round his neck, inscribed with the legend, '*Take care of him. He bites*' (*DC* 81). David's personality appears to be defined by this sample of writing; he is placed at the mercy of readers who will assume that this text is a faithful representation of his real character, leaving him open to unfavourable interpretations and misconstructions that seem to hem him in on all sides: 'What I suffered from that placard, nobody can imagine. Whether it was possible for people to see me or not, I always fancied that somebody was reading it. It was no relief to turn round and find nobody; for wherever my back was, there I imagined somebody always to be' (*DC* 81–2). It does not require too much effort to see in this situation something compatible with the workings of the panopticon. As both narrator and character, David attempts to pre-empt the worst effects of the controlling gaze by usurping the role of surveillance operative himself; as narrator, he surveys himself more than anyone else does; as character, he testifies to the risk of complicity with the more repressive effects of monitoring. It is while he is following Martha through the streets of London, keeping in the shadows all the time so that she cannot see him, that he owns up to a 'strange fascination in the secrecy and mystery of so following anyone' (*DC* 625). Part of the fascination stems from engagement in the whole business of being a surveillance operative, but part of it also inheres in the 'secrecy and mystery' of following not just anyone, but someone who is quite specifically a 'fallen woman'. For a male narrator, restive at the constraints imposed upon him by a given social role, it is the contemplation of a 'fallen woman' that brings with it a sense of relative security and even of complacency. This is because the 'fallen woman' provides some of the most striking examples of a figure whose given social identity is so damaging, which inflicts so much suffering, that, in this text at least, it becomes necessary, if you are a Martha or an Emily, to choose one of two options: either suicide or an active exchange of identities.

For Emily, who at the very least gains the reputation of a 'fallen woman', the only meaningful action to be taken after she has been abandoned by Steerforth is to emigrate, to start life anew, effectively as someone else. This is an active exchange of identities, which has her performing in sequence what the narrator is persistently attempting to develop into a routine in a text that is trying to construct an alibi, to make David the

'Author of his own Being' (*DC* 538) – to adopt a phrase of Micawber – trying to confer authority on a version of the self that conceals more than it reveals, and that conceals precisely what is most significant. And, if Emily is emigrating to Australia, she is moving to a place where the official descriptions of the subject, where the legal definitions that determine relations, are soon to devolve on Mr Micawber in his new capacity as magistrate. Micawber is also making a fresh start, of course, yet he leaves England with 'pecuniary liabilities', adopting an appearance that gives him a 'bold buccaneering air, not absolutely lawless' (*DC* 738) – but very nearly so. As with the emigration to America of Jingle at the end of *The Pickwick Papers*, we cannot be absolutely certain of the final effects of this transplantation.

For Martha, even the prospect of suicide in the river (and the chosen method has to be drowning, of course) brings with it an augmentation of disturbance and distress, not a decrease in or release from everything that degrades her. She identifies herself closely with the river in its most disgusting state:

> 'I know it's like me!' she exclaimed. 'I know that I belong to it. I know that it's the natural company of such as I am! It comes from country places, where there was once no harm in it – and it creeps through the dismal streets, defiled and miserable – and it goes away, like my life , to a great sea, that is always troubled – and I feel that I must go with it!' (*DC* 627)

Martha utters this speech in the slime and decay of a Thames wharf at low tide (it is one of Dickens's great set passages). The setting and her words combine in a way that makes the text's habitual metaphorical resource for forgetting what is unacceptable almost irrevocably tainted with the conditions it is designed to effect an escape from. One might contrast the tenor of this passage with the attitude of the unfallen Emily, who imagines of her drowned father that perhaps 'he had drifted out to them parts, where the flowers is always a-blowing, and the country bright' (*DC* 538); or with David's premonition of the death of Ham, when the latter gazes out on a sea shot through with religious gleams: 'I saw him turn his face towards a strip of silvery light upon the sea, and pass on, looking at it, until he was a shadow in the distance' (*DC* 679). Clearly,

Martha's is a case for which the textual conceit of drowning is simply insufficient to cope with the weight of her experience.

It was during the period immediately preceding the composition of *David Copperfield* that Dickens became closely involved in a scheme for the moral reclamation of prostitutes. Together with the millionairess philanthropist Angela Burdett Coutts, he set up an asylum for fallen women in suburban Shepherd's Bush. Named Urania Cottage, this refuge was run on principles specified minutely by Dickens in two long letters sent to Miss Coutts during the early stages. It is quite clear from these that Dickens took an unusual interest in planning the regime the women were to be submitted to, and in conceiving of its effects. There is no doubt that at some level he relished the control he was able to exert over the women's lives, and the manner in which he chose to exert it. In the earlier of the two letters, dated 26 May 1846 (*L*. iv. 552–6), he can be seen fussing over every last detail of the arrangements for the appointment of staff, the disposition of the furniture, the decorations, the pictures and framed texts to go on the walls, even the range of dress designs. He anticipated with some eagerness the opportunities he would be allowed of policing the women and keeping them under observation. Once the place was established and up and running, he was even capable of acting like a private detective, lurking at street corners in order to spy on the women, especially those suspected of contact with men, which was forbidden. Several women were in fact ejected from the home as a result of his surveillance work. His descriptions of their departure, as for instance in a letter to William Brown, 6 November 1849 (*L*. v. 637–9) reproduce the same combination of sentimental identification with the woman and self-righteous detachment from her designated moral state that characterizes the divisions of purpose within the narrative of *David Copperfield*.

At different times, sometimes at the same time, in the same letter, Dickens saw Urania Cottage in different lights: as a refuge; as a kind of insane asylum; and as an orphanage where he could fill the office of father for all the inmates. He is capable of identifying the root of the problem in a social structure that simultaneously requires and condemns prostitution: 'It is dreadful to think how some of these doomed women have no chance or choice. It is impossible to disguise from one's self the horrible truth that it would have been a social marvel and miracle if some of them had been anything than what they are' (*L.* v. 185). But he is also prone to reach the quite different conclusion that individual women turn to prostitution through an individual susceptibility, which he refers to both as a form of disease and as madness. His understanding of the pathology of prostitution does not correlate with his recognition of its social origins, and renders somewhat superfluous his injunction to the women to practice a kind of self-surveillance: 'You must resolve to set a watch upon yourself, and to restrain yourself' (AFW 698–9).

The method of treatment he decided to adopt was radical, and revolved around an almost brutal insistence on the women's isolation not only from the outside world, but also from their own histories. He was almost obsessed with the idea that the 'power of beginning life anew' could be derived only by cutting the women off from their old associates, and by consigning their past lives to oblivion. It is hardly surprising that a fascination with the idea of forgetting earlier versions of the self should become so pivotal in *David Copperfield*, once we have recognized it as a fixation Dickens could not stop referring to in his plans for Urania Cottage: 'That their past lives should never be referred to, at the Home, there can be no doubt. I should say that any such reference on the part of the Superintendent would be an instance of blind mistake that in itself would render her dismissal necessary' (*L.* v. 182).

The slightly hysterical insistence with which Dickens imposed his conditions on the lives of these women met with no check from Angela Burdett Coutts except in the matter of emigration, which Dickens argued should be the logical sequel to residence in the Home. Miss Coutts was not so sure. But Dickens's plan was to remodel the inmates as potential wives for colonists in those parts of the settled world where women were in short supply. His motivation was informed in part by a shrewd estimate of the number of women who would relapse out of practical necessity if returned to the environment from which they had been saved: 'the streets of London, I confess I view with very great apprehension' (*L.* v. 183). What is especially interesting about Dickens's emigration scheme is the opportunity it afforded him of extending the scope of his influence over the women's development: 'I have provided a form of book, in which we shall keep the history of each case, and which has certain printed enquiries to be filled up by us, before each comes in, and a final blank headed its "Subsequent History", which will remain to be filled up, by degrees, as we shall hear of them, and from them, abroad' (*L.* v. 186). Here, Dickens comes as close as possible to authoring these women's lives, dispatching them to places like Australia, as he does with Martha and Emily at the end of *David Copperfield*, and waiting for them to send him the raw materials to edit, and shape into a coherent form. In this respect, Urania Cottage is another medium in which Dickens can narrate the lives of fallen women.

It is intriguing to speculate about Dickens's own psychology, about his being simultaneously attracted to and repelled by the situation of the fallen woman, but in a sense this is superfluous to the essential point made by the novel in any case in its stress on the kind and scope of damage inflicted on women by prejudice. This is nowhere more effectively demonstrated than in the extraordinary episode that occurs when Emily returns to England and is found in London. The first person actually on the scene is Rosa Dartle, who hurls invective at Emily and then goes through a horrific pantomime of striking at her, as if with an invisible hammer: 'Rosa Dartle sprang up from her seat; recoiled; and in recoiling struck at her, with a face of such malignity, so darkened and disfigured by passion, that I had almost thrown myself between them. The blow, which had no aim, fell upon the air' (*DC* 662). The ugliness of this scene, which locks these two unmarried women into mutually destructive conflict, is a representation of the way in which this particular social formation makes each the most effective agent or instrument of undermining or condemning the other. It presents a challenge that the narrator cannot find a means of dealing with. The two women here confronting each other are placed on either side of a divide that represses the sexuality of the one and outlaws the sexuality of the other; marking the first with the wound of her sex and offering a similar violence to the other. The horrific circularity of their suffering has an effect that lingers in the air of the novel without being dispelled, because it is empowered with all the frustration of a blow that falls upon the air without finding its object. What the narrative attempts to do is to interpose between the two women in the shape of the narrator's surrogate, who almost throws himself between them but does not in fact do so. The rather synthetic figure of Agnes, who resolves all the problems engendered at the level of plot, is surely insufficient to achieve the intended sublimation of the frustrations and damage of womanhood that are here exposed. The centrality of Agnes at the end of the book is a mark of her suitability as the perfect counterpart to the narrator's own alibi of bland civility. As Micawber recognizes in his own attempts to internalize the moral admonitions of Agnes's example, she is really no more than an externalization of the reformed conscience; it is in contemplation of this, he says, that he is stimulated at one and the same time by 'the silent monitor within, and by a no less touching and appealing monitor without'. The vocabulary he uses makes clear the extent to which the union of Agnes and David represents the final attempt to effect a compromise with the conditions of monitoring, or surveillance, that the novel is otherwise so often and so stubbornly in two – and maybe even more than two – minds about.

5

Taking the Roof Off

BLEAK HOUSE*, 'ON DUTY WITH INSPECTOR FIELD', *LITTLE DORRIT

So many of Dickens's texts of the 1840s are built around a tension between two opposing positions: of advantage and disadvantage, control and helplessness. This kind of tension provides the basis of the much more complicated relations of power and knowledge in *Bleak House* (1853). The division of the novel into two narratives leads the reader to anticipate the presentation of two very different ways of apprehending the world and of ordering experience, perhaps along the lines of determining greater or lesser degrees of vantage. One way of approaching these textual relations is by way of two articles written for *Household Words* during the period immediately preceding the composition of the novel: 'Detective Police' (July–August 1850) and 'On Duty with Inspector Field' (June 1851).

The second of these two articles is essentially a piece of reportage, describing the work of the recently formed Detective Police. The most curious and striking aspect of this account is that it barely, and only incidentally, touches on the criminal aspects of their work, presenting them rather as super-constables on the beat, patrolling certain areas of the city, checking up on the inhabitants of the dosshouses around Newgate and St Giles's, the 'tumbling houses' that are no better than infected 'heaps of filth'.The spectacle offered by this text is that of the police as agents of social discipline rather than as catchers of criminals. It is not inappropriate that, in a journal entitled *Household Words*, the police are shown to be engaged in the regulation of households.

The other conspicuous element of this text is its organization into opposing points of view, turning it almost into a miniaturized prototype of *Bleak House*. The narrative point of view follows the police into a variety of buildings in order to see their hidden interiors with the all-powerful eyes of a detective. Once inside, once exposed to the defencelessness of most of the inhabitants, the point of view switches in order to try to imagine the demoralized lives of the inmates of these squalid tenements. The switch is marked by a change from a present tense mode, in which occasional use of the first-person plural alternates with third-person constructions, to the adoption of the first-person singular in order to express the plight of the homeless, lawless, powerless:

> Again, in these confined intolerable rooms, burrowed out like the holes of rats or the nests of insect-vermin, but fuller of intolerable smells, are crowds of sleepers, each on his foul truckle-bed coiled up beneath a rug. Halloa here! Come! Let us see you! Show your face! Pilot Parker goes from bed to bed and turns their slumbering heads towards us, as a salesman might turn sheep. Some wake up with an execration and a threat. – What! Who spoke? O! If it's the accursed glaring eye that fixes me, go where I will, I am helpless. Here! I sit up to be looked at. Is it me you want? Not you, lie down again! And I lie down, with a woful growl.
>
> Wherever the turning lane of light becomes stationary for a moment, some sleeper appears at the end of it, submits himself to be scrutinised, and fades away into the darkness.
>
> There should be strange dreams here, Deputy. They sleep sound enough, says Deputy, taking the candle out of the blacking-bottle, snuffing it with his fingers, throwing the snuff into the bottle, and corking it up with the candle; that's all *I* know. What is the inscription, Deputy, on all the discoloured sheets? A precaution against loss of linen. Deputy turns down the rug of an unoccupied bed and discloses it. STOP THIEF!
>
> To lie at night, wrapped in the legend of my slinking life; to take the cry that pursues me, waking, to my breast in sleep; to have it staring at me, and clamouring for me, as soon as consciousness returns; to have it for my first-foot on New-Year's day, my Valentine, my Birthday salute, my Christmas greeting, my parting with the old year. STOP THIEF!
>
> And to know that I *must* be stopped, come what will. To know that I am no match for this individual energy and keenness, or this organized and steady system! (*SJ* 312)

The grammatical first person, the single, capitalized 'I', is aligned most emphatically with a position of disadvantage, while its homonym, the eye, is aligned with superior vantage. And it is a highly specific eye, represented at one point as a mythological eye: not the multiple organ of Argus, alluded to in *American Notes*, but the very singular eye of the cyclops, that other panopticist who curtailed the liberty, restricted the movements, of Odysseus and his followers: 'Rogers is ready, strapped and great-coated, with a flaming eye [a lamp] in the middle of his waist, like a deformed cyclops' (*SJ* 307). The original cyclops was blinded; Dickens's inclusion of a cyclopean eye at this point suggests a fantasy of blinding, a desire perhaps to share in at least the imagining of an evasion of control.

The cyclopean eye symbolizes control, but the secret of the exercise of power by this means is the application of a system. The detective police are effectively the instruments of an 'organized and steady system'. The phrase thus used in 'On Duty with Inspector Field' has particular resonance in relation to *Bleak House*, where the 'system' as referred to by Gridley is both pernicious and destructively overwhelming. In the Inspector Field text, the idea of system is correlated with organization, methodicalness, rationality, meticulousness, order; all those aspects of police work that remind us that the detectives are officers of the Law, the advance guard of a forensic process that needs to establish connections, link causes to effects, explain motives and consequences – precisely the sort of thing that goes wrong in Chancery, but that is essentially concerned with demonstration, proof, definition, taxonomy.

What one should remember is that a major spectacle of definition and taxonomy had been constructed in London in 1851 and was still in existence: the Great Exhibition. There are both explicit and implicit links between the Inspector Field text and the Great Exhibition; it is actually referred to as early as in the second paragraph. Significantly, *Bleak House* has often been seen by critics as a form of reaction to the Exhibition, because the latter could be seen as a monument of national self-congratulation and complacency that needed somehow undermining and cutting down to size. The point about the Great Exhibition in the context of a discussion about the power of vision is that it presented the rest of the world from the British point of view, surveying all its dominions, dependencies, competitors, and opponents from the imperial panopticon, as it were, and displaying samples of a diversity of cultures, which it described and classified and made understandable from a British perspective. What the Great Exhibition meant was Britain describing the rest of the world in its own terms of reference. In claiming to master the keys to the knowledge of a variety of cultures it was simultaneously expressing its superiority as an imperial power, a power guaranteed by the degree of systematicity and precision, of clarity and consistency, it could give evidence of in its mode of apprehending the world. Its project was dependent on the principle of transparency, a principle embodied literally in the materials used, because the Exhibition was housed in the Crystal Palace, whose walls and roof were made of glass: symbolic of the perspicuousness that surveillance needs to operate effectively. The premium given to transparency in detective work is implied in the etymology of the word 'detection', which means simply 'taking the roof off': *tecta* (Latin)=roof; which is why the board game Cluedo, with its plan of a house, is the quintessence of detection; the roof has been removed (or is see-through, as if made of glass) so that the players can look easily into the various rooms and make the vital connections, solve the case.

The Great Exhibition is not the only national monument to taxonomy referred to in the Inspector Field text, because the British Museum is also mentioned, in the third paragraph. This is the actual location where the *Household Words* correspondent – Dickens himself – encounters Inspector Field for the first time. Precisely what Field is doing in the British Museum, why he is patrolling its corridors and galleries with his lamp in the middle of the night, on the off chance of catching a lurking malefactor, is not all that easy to comprehend. But it does illustrate how strenuous Dickens is in his interest in relating detective work to other forms of definition and taxonomy. This kind of relationship is certainly explored in *Bleak House,* not by means of such simple and bold juxtapositions, but through more intricate and systematic cross-referencing. It is important to try to gauge the hidden scope of detective work in its intimate relationship with the construction of narrative in the fiction of the 1850s and 1860s (the relationship is probably even more intense in the composition of novels by writers like Wilkie Collins). In the other *Household Words* article of this period, the piece entitled simply 'The Detective Police', the relationship could not be more direct; the text records how the majority of inspectors and sergeants from Scotland Yard go in a troop to the office of the editor of *Household Words*, where they sit around in a circle and do nothing but tell stories about their past cases. Detection, here, becomes no more nor less than the pretext for constructing a narrative.

In *Bleak House* itself, there are a host of exemplars, and variants, of detective work, ranging from the specific professionalism of Bucket, through the machinations of Tulkinghorn, to the far less inscrutable, sometimes dramatically unsubtle activities of the minor law-enforcers: the distrainers, the 'follerers', the bailiffs, the Victorian repomen. The eye of the cyclops is there perhaps in the 'villain with one eye', employed to carry out the letter of the law on behalf of Sir Leicester Dedlock, by closing up Boythorn's path; Boythorn wishes to clear away obstructions while Sir Leicester is intent on restoring them: clarity versus obscurity. The power of the eye is also disclosed together with an expression perhaps of a desire to see that power subdued in the circumstances of the Broker's man, Neckett, who operates out of a shop ambivalently named 'Blinders'; he himself is described as a man who is 'never tired of watching'. There are also a great many 'moral policemen', for whom the prototype could be Mrs Pardiggle, the 'inexorable moral Policeman', who is ready to carry everyone 'off to a station-house', and who is characterized, memorably, as having a pair of 'choking eyes'. The eyes of surveillance are as prevalent in this text as in *David Copperfield*, although not yet as ubiquitous as in *Great Expectations*. The monitoring gaze is to be found among many of the named characters, but is also already generally dispersed into the curiosity of the crowd, which is composed of 'outposts of the army of observation'. Attention to these conditions offers also the means of determining the relative status of the various houses described. Chesney Wold is brought to life only in the action, strange to say, of its mirrors (in a chapter entitled 'On the Watch'): 'All the mirrors in the house are brought into action now: many of them after a long blank' (*BH* 188). By contrast, the degradation of Hawdon's (or Nemo's) surroundings in Krook's lodgings is expressed by his dead body being laid open to the 'gaunt eyes in the shutters staring down upon the bed'(*BH* 165). Most notorious of all, the wretched defencelessness that is inseparable from life in Tom-all-Alone's is rapidly conveyed by its characterization as a 'street of perishing blind houses, with their eyes stoned out; without a pane of glass, without so much as a window frame...' (*BH* 120). To pierce or assail others with one's gaze is to assert mastery over them; in order to resist being mastered oneself it is necessary to become impenetrable, inscrutable, one's face an 'expressionless mask' like Tulkinghorn's: he inhabits a room in which 'everything that can have a lock has got one', even though 'no key is visible', where even 'the titles on the backs of his books have retired into the binding'(*BH* 159).

But, of course, these various attempts at imposing discipline hardly ever produce coherence; they are seldom the positive reflections of an 'organized and steady system'. Instead, the 'system', to revert to Gridley's reference, is the producer of chaos and paralysis, obscurity and disease; and clarity and transparency are blotted out in the all-pervading atmosphere of fog and mud. What is proposed immediately in the opening number of the novel is the difficulty of either movement or orientation in the combined fog and mud. The description of the way the mud collects links it to financial investment – it accumulates 'at compound interest' – and links this activity to the conditions of a primeval swamp: 'it would not be wonderful to meet a Megalosaurus' (*BH* 13); even within the first paragraph, the novel has suggested that a society which concentrates on what Carlyle had called the 'cash nexus' is reverting to a primitive form of life. Right at the centre of the fog, at its 'very heart', is Chancery, where the mud in the streets also happens to be at its muddiest; the word 'mud' is different by only one letter from the Chancellor's appellation, 'M'lud'.

From the first few pages of the novel, Chancery is associated with the spread of infection; it 'has its decaying houses and blighted lands in every shire' (*BH* 15), while the court case of Jarndyce and Jarndyce in particular has 'stretched forth its unwholesome hand to soil and corrupt' (*BH* 17) a multitude of unfortunates. In Mr Jarndyce's opinion, the most appalling result of the Great Seal's imprint is the blighting of the lives of children like Jo, who are born and bred in slums like Tom-all-Alone's. This building is at the conceptual heart of the novel, as the alternative and contrasting pivot for its action. Dickens's worksheets show that *Tom-all-Alone's* was his favourite among various titles for the novel that he considered. Practically speaking, it is the source of the infection that Chancery is symbolically responsible for.

The unnamed disease (it is probably smallpox) that Esther contracts is not only a negatively unifying image for the social relations that obtain in the world of *Bleak House*; it is also an accurate index of material conditions in Victorian London. John Ruskin observed that the death rate among the characters in the novel might seem high, and more suitable for a story with a military setting, but argued that this was merely a reflection of a 'properly representative average of the statistics of civilian mortality in the centre of London.'[1] Contagious diseases reached epidemic proportions regularly in the middle years of the nineteenth century; there had been a cholera epidemic only a few years before the composition of *Bleak House*, killing 52,293 people in 1849 alone. There was also growing concern over the practice of 'intra-mural interment' – burial within the city walls – which had sparked a parliamentary inquiry in 1843. This revealed conditions of overcrowding equal to those of the metropolitan graveyard in *Bleak House*.

In these respects, Dickens's portrayal of the 'condition of England' in the novel represents a direct challenge to the England celebrated by the Great Exhibition. Running against the grain of national pride and economic arrogance, the writing in *Bleak House* contemplates the physical and moral deterioration of a population inhabiting an environment that is swathed in the fog of corrupt bureaucracies and paralysed by the weight of inherited problems.

The fog is what joins everything together, but it also separates everything by plunging it into obscurity. It touches everything but makes it simultaneously invisible and unintelligible. In these conditions, the business of everyday life is turned into a system of *un*intelligibilities: 'The town awakes; the great tee-totum is set up for its daily spin and whirl; all that unaccountable reading and writing, which has been suspended for a few hours, recommences. Jo, and the other lower animals, get on in the unintelligible mess as they can' (*BH* 258). It is usually critical aspects of the lives of the poor that have to be left out of the account – that are unaccountable in the organized systems of institutional language. Guster, for example, 'has fits', which the parish cannot account for, and therefore, 'she goes cheap with this unaccountable drawback of fits' (*BH* 156), her convulsions being suggestive of what remains resistant to control, of what will always exceed the official attempts at reduction to order. Esther is convinced that 'I think the best side of such people is almost hidden from us. What the poor are to the poor is little known, excepting to themselves and GOD' (*BH* 135). It is only a character like Boythorn, who has the material resources and the strength of will, of what is in fact a caricature of energy, who is able to expose his character in full: 'it seemed so plain that he had nothing to hide, but showed himself exactly as he was' (*BH* 143). Characters like Tulkinghorn conceal everything out of a jealous fear of slipping from a position of vantage, while the poor remain hidden because the system does not operate with a language that can explain their lives or account for them.

Of course it is Esther's narrative, with its personal tones, and the value it places on emotional truths, that appears to offer to dispel the gloom and supplement the gaps in the impersonal narrator's account. She reaches back over the memories of her life to achieve knowledge and insight, as she says in a comparison she makes herself, shedding light on her experience in a process like that which uncovers the features of a landscape with the breaking of day: 'As the prospect gradually revealed itself, and disclosed the scene over which the wind had wandered in the dark, like my memory over my life, I had a pleasure in discovering the unknown objects that had been around me in my sleep' (*BH* 115). But this is misleading; Esther just as often takes pleasure or relief from leaving things in the dark. Indeed sometimes she takes steps to prevent an accession of lucidity and coherence, to push back into the shadows certain kinds of information that promise to emerge:

> 'I am quite sure that if there were anything I ought to know, [she says to Jarndyce], or had any need to know, I should not have to ask you to tell it to me. If my whole reliance and confidence were not placed in you, I must have a hard heart indeed. I have nothing to ask you; nothing in the world.'

> He drew my hand through his arm, and we went away to look for Ada. From that hour I felt quite easy with him, quite unreserved, quite content to know no more, quite happy. (*BH* 122–3)

The kind of information and awareness she is most concerned to leave unaccountable relates to her sexual identity. She represses her latent sexual feelings for Woodcourt to the extent of displacing him from her accounts of various occasions when he has been present. The high proportion of retrospective mentions turns Woodcourt into quite a ghostly presence for most of the book; the book is well supplied with references to ghosts and spectres, often of the supernatural variety, sometimes with a considerable latitude given to the interpretation of what a ghost is or might be. But ghostliness most frequently suggests an unsatisfied, uncontained, passional life that has to express itself in some residual form. Woodcourt first enters the text out of thin air, materializing suddenly next to the dead Nemo's bed, without anybody noticing the moment or manner of his entrance. Esther's major means of distraction from registering the exchange of glances that must clearly have been engaged in for a good long time before her eventual *rapprochement* with Woodcourt is her heavy overemphasis on the 'languishing eyes' of Guppy that turn him into easily the most persistent surveillance operative in the book. They were 'always gazing at me', records Esther, 'fixed upon me all the evening'; 'So there I sat, not knowing where to look – for wherever I looked, I knew Mr Guppy's eyes were following me' (*BH* 203). But this apparent unease is actually the sign of a rare complacency, because Guppy's responses can be controlled, and Esther's relationship with him is about the only one with a male where she maintains the upper hand.

Much of her first-person account takes the form of deliberately transferring control of her life to others, rather than consisting of a record of initiatives written up in a way that would enable her to maintain and strengthen her hold over her experience. The first-person pronoun is used most intensively in passages that stress Esther's passivity, her compliance with the designs of others, as in the following passage, where a proliferation of first-person pronouns is the result of her enthusiasm at the promise of having her identity almost entirely constructed by the plans of Ada and Richard:

> I was a part of all their plans, for the present and the future. I was to write Richard once a week, making my faithful report of Ada, who was to write to him every alternate day. I was to be informed, under his own hand, of all his labours and successes; I was to observe how resolute and persevering he would be; I was to be Ada's bridesmaid when they were married; I was to live with them afterwards; I was to be made happy for ever and a day. (*BH* 215)

The curious effect of this passage is that, despite the proliferation of 'I's, it renders a sense of Esther as someone detached from her own self – almost as if she is writing about a third person; like Skimpole – only with a very different motivation, of course – 'speaking of himself as if he were not at all his own affair, as if Skimpole were a third person' (*BH* 90).

If Esther's motivation in appending herself to the development of relationships between others is a denial of her own sexuality, this must be rooted partly in the influence of her guardian, who filled her youth with obscure condemnations of extra-marital sex and who died of a seizure when Esther had been on the verge of reading aloud the biblical passage about the woman taken in adultery. Still in her adolescence, she welcomes the use of nicknames to characterize her as an old woman, as if she is already past the age of active sexuality. Before Woodcourt effects a conversion of her nature that is not properly accounted for, she shows most interest in men who pose no challenge sexually, either because they are effeminate, like Prince Turveydrop, or paternal, like Jarndyce.

The critical juncture of Esther's life, and certainly of her narrative, is the fever from which she emerges with a pock-marked face. This disfigurement is all of a piece with the interest in *David Copperfield* in women who are facially scarred or wounded. The hammer blow on the face of Rosa Dartle and the disfigurement of Esther suggest a cancelling-out of their sexuality at the same time that their afflictions register the force of the psychological pressures that lead to the necessity of that cancelling. Esther ends up with a pock-marked face because in some sense she needs to, while at the same time her vividly physical self-effacement counts the cost of the first person's submission to the 'organized and steady system' of Dickens's social world.

But even while *Bleak House* understands the penalties of incorporation into the vast impersonal systems of social discipline, it also tries to wish them away at the end. *Little Dorrit* (1857) is almost equally fraught with anxiety in this connection, but locates freedom from the pressures of regulation in the most unlikely zones. While Esther keeps the keys to a household she will eventually preside over, Amy Dorrit has the clue of access to a much more ambiguous building, or set of buildings, the Marshalsea. The Marshalsea is contradistinctive to the majority of prison structures, including certain imaginative structures, in Dickens's writings, being the opposite of panoptical. Consisting of a block of urban dwellings run into one another to form a single unit, the Marshalsea is an incoherent assemblage of various buildings accommodating a series of separate households. It is a knowable community, tucked away in a recess of the emphatically unknowable London, fostering a degree of mutual dependence among the prisoners of a sort that cannot be sustained outside its walls. According to the inmate Dr Haggage, it is a haven of peace and freedom, insulating its little community against the attritions of everyday economic life. Above all it is a family prison, preserving the value of family relations and organizing itself spontaneously into an extended family structure in which the natural authority figure is neither a governor, nor a warder, but an inmate, William Dorrit, the 'Father of the Marshalsea'.

It is in this milieu that Amy Dorrit is found; indeed, she has been born and brought up there, a Wordsworthian child who has sprung not from the requisite proximity to Nature, but from the hugely paradoxical environment of an urban gaol. It is an extraordinary indictment of the British social system that moral integrity should be endangered by it, and should need protection from it in the shape of an institution whose ostensible purpose is to punish the immoral. Outside the Marshalsea, the project of identity is virtually unsustainable; characters are portrayed routinely as psychologically damaged or incomplete. As in much fiction of Dickens's mature period, there is a fixation on doubling and division, on the scarcity of examples of successful social individuation. The potency of references to twins and other symbolic pairs of characters – Pet Meagles and her dead sister, the two versions of Mr Flintwich that make

Affery's head go 'round and round' – is the extent to which they suggest the reality and power of denied and repressed components of the self. Tattycoram's social function is to act as substitute for the missing twin, but the performance of that role depends on the paradoxical elision of aspects of her own character. This involves a degree of destructive force that only a campaign of physical self-abuse can begin to indicate:

> 'My poor girl, what is the matter?'
>
> She looked up suddenly, with reddened eyes, and with her hands suspended, in the act of pinching her neck, freshly disfigured with great scarlet blots. 'It's nothing to you what's the matter. It don't signify to anyone.' (*LD* 64)

Contrary to her belief, the red blotches signify to everyone attentive to Esther's pock-marks, or to Miss Dartle's scar. They are the body's fault-lines, the cracks in the edifice that record the process of forging the self. It is the vocabulary of forging, of both shaping and falsifying the self, that Dickens employs in his second great essay in first-person fiction. The alternative careers of blacksmith and gentleman shadow each other constantly in the language of *Great Expectations.*

6

The Stupendous Power of Money

GREAT EXPECTATIONS, AUTOBIOGRAPHICAL FRAGMENT

Great Expectations (1861) was the last of Dickens's weekly serials. The huge pressures attendant on serialization, which Dickens had been finding more and more burdensome in the course of his development as a monthly serialist, were suddenly enhanced at this fairly late stage in his career. He had been feeling the need for more time to devote to thinking about and planning his novels, and now he found himself with less. *A Tale of Two Cities,* the novel that immediately preceded *Great Expectations,* had also been a weekly serial, and Dickens had been so unsettled by the constrictions of the weekly instalment that he wrote to Forster in August 1859 that 'nothing in the mere way of money... could also repay the time and trouble of the incessant condensation' (*L.* ix. 112). During the composition of *Great Expectations,* he further complained to Forster that: 'As to the planning out from week to week, nobody can imagine what the difficulty is without trying' (*L.* ix. 403).

'Nothing in the mere way of money', according to Dickens in 1859, could compensate for the ordeal of weekly serialization. And yet it was not simply a reduction in the temporal scale of the instalments of work required to produce the text of *Great Expectations* that exerted a peculiar pressure on Dickens at this time, because the book was conceived of and written in circumstances that intensified the usual financial imperative that lay behind Dickens's work. The immediate stimulus to the composition of the book was in fact a very urgent need to make money. He needed it to revive the flagging fortunes of his new periodical *All the Year Round*, which had started successfully with the serial publication of *A Tale of Two Cities*, in April 1859, and which had been sustained by the extraordinary popularity of Wilkie Collins's *The Woman in White*, but which had started to nose-dive with the publication of Charles Lever's *A Day's Ride*. Sales began to drop, as Dickens had anticipated they might, and he saw no alternative but to contribute a new novel of his own. 'It was perfectly clear', he told Forster, 'that the one thing to be done was, for me to strike in. I have therefore decided to begin the story as of the length of the *Tale of Two Cities* on the first of December'; 'by dashing in now, I come in when most wanted' (*L*. ix. 319–20). The gambit paid off in every sense, so that, by the time Dickens was writing the concluding numbers in July and August 1861, circulation had gone up to about 100,000.

Thematically, *Great Expectations* places a sceptical emphasis on what Pip at one stage calls 'the stupendous power of money', and yet the very conditions in which the book was produced were such as to accord a due amount of respect to this power. The urgency of Dickens's response to it can be seen in the tension generated by the demands of weekly composition and publication. Much of the novel's material is concerned with the venality to be found at every level of the society that the writing portrays; but there are other ways in which the economic necessity of the weekly tempo of the writing works its way into the text. I am not primarily thinking of those aspects of the writing that respond most obviously to the periodical rhythms of composition: the element of suspense, for example, typically illustrated by the assault on Pip's sister, Mrs Joe, reported at the end of chapter 15 and often cited by critics as a classic example of the use of suspense in serialization; nor am I thinking of the timeliness, or topicality, that Dickens introduces into his text – for example, in the December numbers, when he deals with a series of events leading up to the melodramatic interruption of a Christmas dinner; what I am more concerned with are the ways in which the urgent passing of time – the urgently demoralizing passing of time – is figured in the text.

Nearly everything Pip finds threatening or disheartening can be linked to an emphasis on the passing of time, or, more specifically, to the action of clocks and watches. Near the beginning of the text, we are introduced from the point of view of the young Pip to the strange clicking noise that Magwitch makes in his throat; to Pip, the noise makes him seem 'as if he had works in him like a clock, and was going to strike' (*GE* 50). The connection between the passing of time and the disruption of private life, of a self-contained world, is first made incidentally here; but it establishes a pattern that the rest of the novel traces out assiduously. Pip's first real introduction to the predatoriness of the public world is made through the figure of the odious Mr Pumblechook, who supplies the Sergeant in charge of the soldiers pursuing Magwitch with the exact time, 'just gone half-past two' – a marking of time that might seem gratuitous, but that is supposed to demonstrate the extent to which Pumblechook is 'a man whose appreciative powers justified the inference that he was equal to the time' (*GE* 62). What the reader is intended to infer here is that Pumblechook is in more than one sense equal to the time: his hypocritical self-serving is characteristic of the times he lives in, and he is one of those who measures, or regulates, or is even in control of, the time everyone has to live by. Far more daunting than Pumblechook, however, far more in control than he is, is the stupendously powerful Jaggers, who knows the exact value of time, who never does anything unless he is paid to do it; who runs his life, and the lives of others, according to a rigid timetable – turning his dinner guests out at half-past nine sharp, whether they are ready to disperse or not. Jaggers is a daunting figure who strikes fear into the hearts of both adversaries and clients; his power is most simply and visibly conveyed in the way he flaunts his gold repeater watch with its massive chain – a watch that no thief would ever dare attempt to steal. It is in fact described awkwardly, and therefore pointedly, as a 'thief-dreaded' watch, and is perhaps the most conspicuous indication of how an association with the passing of time represents an ability to manipulate the lives of others.

Of course, the polar opposite to the worldliness of these men, or so it would seem, the most striking exception to their rule of involvement in the tide of affairs, is the reclusive and obsessive Miss Havisham, for whom time is completely frozen, whose clocks have all stopped and whose shuttered windows never allow the alternation of day and night or the differentiation of the seasons to announce themselves, who remains fantastically in the attitude of her wedding day – one shoe off and one shoe on, even though the stocking on her unshod foot has been worn to tatters. Miss Havisham is a character who is developed according to the rhythms of weekly serialization and yet she does not know, as she says, 'anything' of the days of the week – she cannot tell one from another. If Jaggers and Pumblechook are linked with the remorseless aspect of the passing of time, Miss Havisham is no less remorseless in her attempt to elude the passing of time; if the paraphernalia of her shrouded rooms – her yellowing clothes and rotting bridal cake – do not sufficiently suggest the grotesque sterility of the timelessness she aims at, Pip spells it out when he takes stock of her situation immediately after the marriage of Estella to Drummle: 'in shutting out the light of day, she had shut out infinitely more; in seclusion, she had secluded herself from a thousand natural and healing influences; her mind, brooding solitary, had grown diseased, as all minds do and must and will that reverse the appointed order of their Maker' (*GE* 411). Pip sounds very knowing, but his statement reflects ironically both on his own situation and on his understanding of the order of things in general. The book is absolutely filled with would-be 'makers': those who usurp and pervert the divine prerogative of creation, the making of human beings; they try to make human beings into what they are not. Magwitch tries to make Pip; Miss Havisham tries to make Estella; Jaggers stands in the relation of creator to creature with regard to Molly and a host of other unfortunates and felons; Pip himself makes the Avenger, tries to make Herbert, and even appears willing to make the second Pip, son of Biddy and Joe, at the end of the book. The inevitable sequence of 'do and must and will' is expressive of the pattern these makers wish to impose on the lives of those they have adopted or taken possession of. And Pip's statement is even more directly ironic, since his judgement of Miss Havisham's mistakes is one that he might pass on himself, because both before and after he draws these conclusions about her experience, he repeats, admittedly to a less spectacular degree, some of the same mistakes that she makes.

When Magwitch re-enters his life – before Pip makes this statement – the inevitable sequence of his career as seemingly dictated by his 'great expectations' is replaced by temporal disorientation: 'As to forming any plan for the future, I could as soon have formed an elephant... I thought how miserable I was, but hardly knew why, or how long I had been so, or on what day of the week I made the reflection, or even who I was that made it' (*GE* 344). Like Miss Havisham, Pip gets into a state where he cannot tell one day of the week from another, as a result of his own conception of temporal sequence coming into conflict with the temporal sequence conceived for him by his 'maker' – his human maker, that is: Magwitch. The idea of the lack of synchronization this entails is introduced just before Magwitch enters Pip's lodgings by the syncopated striking of the hour by the city churches: 'I read with my watch upon the table, purposing to close my book at eleven o'clock. As I shut it, Saint Paul's, and all the many church-clocks in the City – some leading, some accompanying, some following – struck that hour. The sound was curiously flawed by the wind' (*GE* 331–2). The order of Pip's life, an order regulated by his own watch, is contested with the arrival of Magwitch, and the striking of the same hour at different times by different churches perhaps suggests how this city is not coordinated, is not in line with an 'appointed' order, but is in fact subject to the conflicting orders of different 'makers', all in competition with one another.

In spite of appearances, in spite of what he says, Pip never really revises this situation, or his understanding of it, to the extent that one might expect. After the much more serious disorientation of his nervous breakdown, and after Joe has nursed him back to health, he makes the fatal mistake of trying to reverse the order of time, believing that he can return to the village of his childhood and find Biddy as ready and willing to take up with him as she had been about five years before – before he had turned his back on her. And the extent to which his return to the scenes of his childhood can be represented as regressive is suggested by the eagerness of his identification with the second Pip, whom he initially refers to as 'I again'. In the final scenes covered by his narrative, Pip can be seen unmistakably trying to arrest the clock.

Setting himself to reap the commercial advantages of weekly serialization also exposed Dickens constantly to the agonizing sense of running out of time. What the situation of having to write in weekly bursts with the idea of keeping and enlarging the audience also exposed him to was an excruciating sense of having to work constantly under the public gaze, of not being able to make even the slightest move without being aware of the likely public reaction to it. To an unusually acute degree, Dickens must have been aware of a readership that was watching and waiting for the outcome of every artistic decision he made. The sense of being laid open to public scrutiny is inherent thoughout the entire text of *Great Expectations*, so it is important to indicate how sensitive Dickens is likely to have been to the kind of feelings of vulnerability and nakedness involved. In the 'Autobiographical Fragment' that Dickens supplied to his first biographer, John Forster, the whole humiliating episode of his employment in Warren's Blacking is brought to a crisis by nothing more nor less than Dickens's having had to work under the public gaze. He and his workmate Bob Fagin were set to work in the window giving onto Bedford Street and, because of their dexterity, 'sometimes there would be quite a little crowd there'.[1] The sense of shame and degradation attached to this experience is impossible to ignore, since Dickens adds immediately that 'I saw my father coming in at the door one day when we were very busy, and I wondered how he could bear it.'[2] The quarrel between his father and his employer that led to his dismissal from Warren's Blacking is also rooted, as far as Dickens is concerned, in this business of being exposed to public view: 'It may have had some backward reference, in part, for anything I know, to my employment at the window.'[3] Dickens does not in fact know, which makes his calculated guess an extremely revealing one. Just as with *Great Expectations*, where the reader has constantly to take the measure of the difference in attitude between the young Pip and the adult narrator, so with the 'Autobiographical Fragment' the reader has to remain constantly aware that Dickens's interpretation of events in his childhood is coloured by his continuing pre-occupations as an adult.

Within the text of *Great Expectations* itself, there is a remarkable passage in which the commercial basis of society is accounted for entirely in terms of supervising and being supervised:

Mr Pumblechook appeared to conduct his business by looking across

> the street at the saddler, who appeared to transact his business by keeping his eye on the coachmaker, who appeared to get on in life by putting his hands in his pockets and contemplating the baker, who in turn folded his arms and stared at the grocer, who stood at his door and yawned at the chemist. (*GE* 84)

What is remarkable is that the single exception to this, the only man who is exempted from this process of mutual inspection, is a man who is seen at work in the window of his shop, under the public gaze. It is a striking transformation of the most humiliating episode of Dickens's youth, that this figure should not be having to prove himself 'equal to the time', as Pumblechook has to in his pursuit of wealth, nor is he subject to the atrocious deadlines that Dickens the weekly serialist is; he is in fact someone who, rather than being controlled by time, is himself, at least by implication, in control of time, because he is a watchmaker: 'The watch-maker, always poring over a little desk with a magnifying glass at his eye, and always inspected by a group of smock-frocks poring over him through the glass of his shop-window, seemed to be about the only person in the High-street whose trade engaged his attention' (*GE* 84). What this local conceit offers is the suggestion that being in control of time – and the control in this instance is a symbolic one – is to be associated with a sublime indifference to the stares, the 'poring over', the almost unbroken scrutiny of others that lies at the basis of every kind of commercial transaction in this society. In the text of *Great Expectations* as a whole, there is an almost incessant registering of being haunted by the image of faces that have their eyes fixed on you.

There is almost too much material that is illustrative of this emphasis, but it is necessary to indicate the extent of its hold over the text. In the initial episode of Pip's encounter with Magwitch, it is the boy's fear of being spotted and caught in the act of stealing on behalf of the convict that is constantly focused on, so that the terrified boy is convinced that even the cattle are 'staring' at him 'out of their eyes' and that 'one black ox, with a white cravat on – who even had to my awakened conscience something of a clerical air – fixed me so obstinately with his eyes, and moved his blunt head round in such an accusatory manner as I moved round, that I blubbered out to him, "I couldn't help it, sir! It wasn't for myself I took it!"'(*GE* 48). After Magwitch's arrest, the next serious disturbance to Pip is occasioned by the 'aiming eye' of the ex-convict who turns up in the village at Magwitch's request to pay Pip the two one-pound notes. On his second visit to Satis House, Pip is made to stand in a window, in a 'very uncomfortable state of mind' (*GE* 108), while he is inspected disapprovingly by the relatives of Miss Havisham. Already ashamed at having been seen crying by Estella, once he becomes an apprentice blacksmith, he starts to be 'haunted by the fear' that one day he should 'lift up my eyes and see Estella looking in at one of the wooden windows of the forge' (*GE* 136). Once again, the fear of being overseen at work carries with it the apprehension of being exposed to a gaze that would 'exult over me and despise me' (*GE* 136).

After the revelation of his 'great expectations', Pip begins to resent the idea of being looked at, in his transformed state, by his old acquaintances. With his new set of clothes ordered, he considers that 'it would be very disagreeable to be stared at by all the people here'. But even in the town, his new get-up makes him feel miserably conspicuous, 'suspicious after all that I was at a personal disadvantage, something like Joe's in his Sunday suit' (*GE* 183). On a subsequent return visit to the town, he actually goes two miles out of his way in order to avoid the resentful, predatory gaze of Mr Pumblechook, only to have to suffer an experience of 'inexpressible terror, amazement, and indignation' (*GE* 266) when he is turned into a laughing-stock through the antics of Trabb's boy, reduced to a state of powerlessness that is enhanced to the degree to which he is made a spectacle.

Once he gets to London, the feeling of being under surveillance is intensified, so that, when he is waiting in Jaggers's office, he is conscious even of 'the distorted adjoining houses looking as if they had twisted themselves to peep down at me through' the skylight (*GE* 188). Resting on the shelves in Jaggers's office are the plaster casts of the two 'brutal clients' that periodically excite Pip's self- consciousness. And he finds he is able to enjoy his first dinner in London only 'when the waiter was not there to watch me'.

Pip himself exhorts Herbert to counteract the pressure that begins to rule both their lives in the shape of mounting debts, by responding in kind to the usual, optical means of being called to account: '"Look the thing in the face"', advises Pip, '"Look into your affairs. Stare them out of countenance." "So I would,

Handel,"' replies Herbert, '"only they are staring *me* out of countenance"' (*GE* 295–6).

Once Magwitch reappears, of course, Pip's paranoia is subject to an exponential increase, and he never ceases to stress, one way or another, how 'difficult it is in a large city to avoid the suspicion of being watched' (*GE* 356). From this point until the end of the book, Pip's chief concern is ostensibly to keep Magwitch hidden, away from the prying eyes that might be gathering information to lead to his arrest and trial. But what really obsesses Pip, more than his alarm at the idea of eyes prying at Magwitch, is the idea of eyes continuing to pry at himself: 'I could not', he admits, 'get rid of the notion of being watched' (*GE* 393). And of course the pair of eyes that is fixed on Pip much more than any other pair, the eyes which can never get enough of Pip, which can never drink their fill of him, are none other than the eyes of Magwitch himself: 'All I stip'late, is, to stand by and look at you, dear boy!' (*GE* 346). Pip is horrified by the revelation that for years Magwitch has been motivated by 'looking at' Pip in his mind's eye, and anticipating the moment when he could look at him in the flesh. In his relationship with Magwitch more than in any other, Pip's fear of being watched is irreversibly correlated with a feeling of powerlessness, of being in the control of whoever it is doing the watching, and he is suddenly made to realize that 'for weeks gone by, I had passed faces in the streets which I had thought like his' (*GE* 341). From this point on, he sees eyes in the wall, eyes in lamps, eyes everywhere.

And Pip is not the only character in the book who is demoralized by this feeling of being on display or at the visual disposal of others. When Jaggers compels Molly to display herself and the state of her wrists before the assembled dinner company she begs for remission; and when she fails to get it, her only resort is to return the intensity of the onlookers' gaze by 'turning [her eyes] watchfully on every one of the rest of us in succession' (*GE* 236). Miss Havisham, of course, provides only a more extreme version of Pip's own tendency to retreat from the gaze: the windows of her house are shuttered and barred, she discourages visitors and allows only a minimum of artificial light, preferring to move around her house at night when nobody else is around to watch.

The inevitable concomitant of this sense of being held in place and controlled by being the object of a pointed attention is a feeling of guilt and even of criminality. Pip reveals that he has always had the feeling that he must have been regarded as a young offender even at birth. And when he is trapped into helping Magwitch, he is forced to choose between the alternatives of treason and betrayal: treason towards the king, or the laws of the land, or betrayal of a fellow human being; either way, he is caught in a double bind from which any outcome is going to induce in him a sense of guilt. Thereafter, he is prone to see himself almost as innately criminal. After he has been challenged to a boxing match by the 'pale young gentleman' Herbert, and after he has beaten him, his primary concern is to remove the evidence of his crime, to 'wash out that evidence of my guilt' (*GE* 122). When he is bound apprentice to Joe, he is propelled through the streets by Pumblechook, who holds him 'all the while as if we had looked in on our way to the scaffold' (*GE* 133). Pip is painfully conscious of being the centre of attention, miserably aware of the rapidity with which the onlookers assume that he is some kind of malefactor: 'I heard some people say, "What's he done?" and others, "he's a young 'un, too, but looks bad, don't he?"' (*GE* 132). The assumption that Pip is always in the wrong is made by others, but it is made by him as well. When Mr Wopsle reads the 'affecting tragedy of George Barnwell' to Pip and Mr Pumblechook, his two seniors have no trouble in identifying Pip with the murderous apprentice; but when, shortly afterwards, it is discovered that Mrs Joe has been assaulted, Pip himself, with his head full of George Barnwell, is impelled to confess that 'I was at first disposed to believe that *I* must have had some hand in the attack upon my sister' (*GE* 147).

Once again, it is not only Pip who is prone to introject these accusatory glances, these attributions of guilt, and to find within himself a chord that can be struck in response to the suspiciousness he reads in the eyes of others. Even Herbert, the transparently honest and innocent Herbert, after having been exposed to the searching scrutiny of Jaggers is prepared to say of himself that 'he thought he must have committed a felony and forgotten the details of it, he felt so dejected and guilty' (*GE* 311).

When Pip is marched to the Town Hall by Mr Pumblechook, in order to be bound apprentice to Joe, one of the bystanders, thinking he is a criminal who needs to be reclaimed, thrusts into his hand a religious tract that is inscribed 'TO BE READ IN MY CELL'. Although Pip is not about to be literally incarcerated, there is an important sense in which this aligning of a judgemental regard, and of a corresponding wave of anxiety in which one is forced to regard oneself as culpable, with the use of a metaphor of imprisonment, can be extended and applied to the general condition of society that is depicted in the text. It is not too much to say that everyone is in prison to the extent that he or she reacts to the force of the accusatory regard. Several critics, most notably Jeremy Tambling, have explored that aspect of *Great Expectations* that responds to the notion of surveillance as an instrument of control and suppression in the context of a system of imprisonment; and the system of imprisonment they have in mind is that of the panopticon. Such arguments have a general relevance when applied to a text that is so well supplied with references to prisons: to Newgate, to the prison hulks in the Thames, to the life of a transported convict. But there are also some unusually specific references to panopticism in *Great Expectations.*

The original panopticon, consisting of the hundred eyes of *Argos Panoptes*, who was set to guard Io against rape but who failed and was metamorphosed into the eyes on the peacock's tail, is present in the text in the form of the night-light that is given to Pip in the Hummums, which is where he is forced to sleep when it is made clear to him, in the words of Wemmick, that his own home 'had been watched, and might be watched again' (*GE* 383). The description of the night light is given in terms that link it unmistakably with the disciplinary apparatus to be found in panoptical prisons; the light is a rush light, 'placed in *solitary confinement* at the bottom of a *high* tin *tower*, perforated with round holes that make a *staringly wide-awake* pattern on the walls.' (*GE* 380; emphases added.) This extraordinary contraption, which Pip calls a 'foolish Argus' (*GE* 380), recalls quite overtly the principles on which Bentham's design for the panopticon was based.

But, despite the suggestiveness of this decription, it is important to stress how the unity of surveillance with imprisonment has sometimes been overemphasized, to an extent that has meant displacing an equal emphasis within the text on the links between looking, staring, supervising, and involvement in those processes that are activated by the 'stupendous power of money'. The only actual building in *Great Expectations* that is organized around panoptical principles is not a prison at all, nor is it one of those buildings that resembles a prison without being one; it is rather a building that is entirely given over to financial transactions of the most abstract kind: it is a counting house, the institution that Herbert is rather fictitiously employed at; not a particularly successful counting house, but one that is organized according to the methods that underpin the fiction's entire social system. The counting house is described as an *Observatory*, a place where, if one wants to be successful in capitalist terms, one goes in order to 'look about one'. Capitalism, according to Herbert's practice, and also according to the seedsman, the coach-maker, the saddler, the baker, the grocer, and the chemist, to name only those we have been told about, depends for its continuing existence on the maintenance of a kind of mutual supervising, animated by an indefatigable desire to know precisely what it is your opposite number would never want to own up to.

And as for those buildings that are described as resembling prisons and strongholds, it needs to be stressed that what makes them look carceral, or the reasons their occupants have for turning them into impregnable fortresses, do not so much constitute a desire on the inmates' part to lock themselves in as to lock the world of staring and supervising out. Satis House and Wemmick's Castle are reminiscent of prisons, but their chief purpose is to resist the principles on which the panopticon is based. Satis House even disallows the medium of light; its windows are all barred and shuttered or walled up, in order to prevent the observer from penetrating to the secret existence that is endured within. Wemmick's Castle sports every appearance of being heavily fortified and impenetrable; it even has a drawbridge and cannon. But it is the extent to which it is successful in keeping the world of Little Britain out that determines the quality of its atmosphere of refreshment and relaxation. Nobody can get in except by invitation or by working one of the secret levers that announces the arrival to the Aged

Parent of either 'John' or 'Miss Skiffins'. And it seems very pointed that, immediately after Pip has spent his agonizing night at the Hummums in the company of his own personal panopticon, he should resort to Wemmick's Castle and be a witness of the possibilities that survive there of leading an essentially private life. Pip arrives before the Aged Parent has got out of bed, but, in this haven of self-reliance and self-suffiency, not only is it impossible to be embarrassed by the possibility of making a spectacle of oneself, it is even just for a moment supposed to be impossible to be seen at all, in any way that would would make one feel uncomfortable: 'there seemed to be a tacit understanding', reports Pip, 'that the Aged was not in a presentable state, and was therefore to be considered invisible' (*GE* 383).

What Wemmick is trying to provide a polar opposite to in Walworth is the world of the symbolically named Little Britain, the locale in which Jaggers's office is sited. Jaggers's office is the imaginative hub around which revolves the world of the stupendous power of money; Pip records his impression that when Jaggers is in court he seems to be 'grinding the whole place in a mill', reducing the complex mixture of truths and falsehoods, guilt and innocence, justice and injustice, to the single constituent that represents simply what he will have to do in order to be paid. Wemmick, in his office mood, celebrates his employer's professional lack of discrimination between the morality and the solvency of his clients and indicates the destructive scope of that lack of distinction in his jubilant claim that Jaggers actually possesses them 'body and soul'. The business that is transacted in their office repeats the division between watchers and those who are watched but heightens the tension of this opposition into an altercation between those who 'beat' and those who 'cringe'. This categorizing of human beings as either the agents or the patients of victimization is relevant to the vast majority of relationships depicted in the book. Even Wemmick, whose mercenary habits the reader is tempted to think are assumed, shows that he has a basically imperturbable fixation on the necessity to extort 'portable property' from anyone he has even a modicum of power or influence over. And while Pip's introduction to the world beyond the forge involves him in a devastating discovery of the unequal basis of all relationships, not just of the relationship between his sister and Joe, which he already knows about, his opening up to the possibilities of escaping from a more passive and disadvantaged position within the class system merely draws him into a more subtle and insidious version of the same enthralment; his fascination with Estella starts to develop over a game of cards with the resonant name of 'beggar my neighbour', and the parallel between Estella's treatment of Pip and Jaggers's treatment of his clients is drawn when Pip tells us that he worships the very hem of Estella's dress, thus calling to mind the despair and humiliation of the Jewish client who dances around Jaggers, repeatedly kissing the hem of his garment but to no avail.

Pip is more than once portrayed as being as abject as a dog in the presence of Estella, and the degradation that this suggests is compounded into something much more brutal in the reminder it gives of Magwitch's driven state on the marshes, where his behaviour when eating seems to Pip indistinguishable from that of a starving and distrustful dog. Pip himself is fed in the yard of Satis House by Estella in what he himself describes as a doglike manner, but the psychological cruelty that this is a manifestation of seems to be more tellingly pointed in the comparison between Estella and Pip and the figures of an eagle and a lamb. This makes Pip the victim of a predator, an instinctive killer; and so it comes as something of a shock when, at the end of the book, he himself is charged with possessing the character of a wolf by none other than Dolge Orlick, who seems on the face of it to be one of the most predatory and violent characters in the entire novel. If Pip is a wolf in relation to Orlick, then the basis on which savagery is attributed to a character can be established only in respect of his or her command of the power that accrues to the possession of 'great expectations'. Because Pip has these, he has only to say the word and Orlick can be deprived of his livelihood.

The really basic struggle for survival that underlies the competitiveness that motivates so many of the characters in this novel leads to an extremely high proportion of references to physical violence. Jaggers is said by Wemmick to be constantly regarding his clients as a form of prey: '"Always seems to me," said Wemmick, "as if he had set a man-trap and was watching it.

Suddenly – click – you're caught"' (*GE* 221). (One way or another, 'click' becomes one of the most sinister sounds in the novel.) Jaggers's office in Little Britain is conspicuously juxtaposed with the incessant spectacle of slaughter that is offered by Smithfield, that 'shameful place, all asmear with filth and fat and blood and foam' (*GE* 189). His own name, which echoes the German word for hunter, *jäger*, suggests perhaps a sharp or cutting edge, and it is extremely similar to the special term 'jigger', which Orlick is particularly fond of employing. Pip provides a unique etymology of this word, which he says is meant to 'convey an idea of something savagely damaging. When I was younger, I had had a general belief that if he had jiggered me personally, he would have done it with a sharp and twisted hook' (*GE* 158). It is quite outstanding how much of the text, especially in the early chapters dealing with Pip's childhood sensibility, is almost saturated with images of mutilation and cannibalistic aggression. Magwitch's initial threat to Pip is that the mysterious young man will tear out his heart and liver, and he himself vows to pull down Compeyson like a bloodhound. When the soldiers arrive and give chase to Magwitch himself, the anticipation of a blood sport is what gives the guests at the Gargerys' Christmas dinner an almost cannibalistic pleasure in their meal: 'they were enjoying themselves so much,' considers Pip, 'I thought what terrible good sauce for a dinner my fugitive friend on the marshes was' (*GE* 64). Pumblechook has already forced Pip to imagine himself in the place of the pig that has been slaughtered to provide the dinner, and Mrs Joe has invited her husband to think of himself as a stuck pig.

Miss Havisham's anticipation of what will happen once she has died involves her surviving relatives coming to feast upon her: 'Sharper teeth than teeth of mice have gnawed me' (*GE* 117) she cautions, referring obliquely to the great disappointment of her life. She in turn gloats over the potential havoc she may be able to wreak among men through the medium of Estella with a constantly reiterated 'greediness' in the attitude she shows towards her young charge: she dotes on her creation with a 'ravenous intensity' (*GE* 261), attempting to engross her attention, 'as though she were devouring the beautiful creature she had reared' (*GE* 320); just as Magwitch reproduces his 'ravenous' and 'greedy' manner of eating, 'like a hungry old dog' (*GE* 346), in the moment when he comes to claim the possession of his very own 'brought-up London gentleman'; and just as Orlick, once he is convinced that Pip is firmly and finally within his grasp, draws his hand across his mouth, 'as if his mouth watered for me' (*GE* 436).

What these figurings of violent appetitiveness and hints of cannibalism underscore is the destructive impulse that accompanies and completes the urge to create others, not exactly in one's own image, but in the image of what one was unable to become oneself. This holds good for both Magwitch and Miss Havisham, who, from varying motives, both destroy certain aspects of the personalities of Pip and Estella in attempting to incorporate them into the patterns of their own lives. The passionate intensity with which they pursue their designs is hopelessly mingled with a perverted or misdirected form of love. And it is the apparent hopelessness of the attempt to preserve that love, in the context of an intention to wreak revenge on a world that has trapped them into relationships in which the only possible alternatives are those of being a beater and a cringer, that creates in many of the other characters an almost automatic divorce between the side of one's nature that deals with feeling and that which has to do with power and commerce. The most schematic example of this is provided by Wemmick, for whom 'the office is one thing, and private life is another' (*GE* 231), and who seems to metamorphose, even physically, as he moves from one locale to the other. In the office, his face appears rigid and wooden and his mouth is regularly described as resembling a postbox, as if to advertise that any communication he enters into in his office style will be carried on as if over a great distance. But at Walworth he is tender towards the Aged Parent, devoted to Miss Skiffins, and self-sacrificing in pursuit of Pip's best interests. Dickens is careful to prevent his becoming merely a figure of eccentricity and quaintness by dwelling on the inconsistency of his dual role as gardener: first as the provider of sustenance, a life-giving gardener, in Walworth, and then in Newgate, which is dubbed Wemmick's greenhouse, and where it strikes Pip that 'Wemmick walked among the prisoners, much as a gardener might walk among his plants' (*GE* 280–1). The set of terms that allows the prisoners to be conceived of as starved and dying plants, the objects of unnatural treatment, is transferred direct from the description of the Fleet prison in *The Pickwick Papers*. The note of sobriety that it adds to the reader's appreciation of the role of Wemmick is turned almost sour on the occasion of his penultimate appearance in the book, when he is in the office and turns with an unprecedented savagery on a hapless client; it is a display of aggression, which he relishes, and is sustained by, as much as Jaggers; they both go back to 'work again with an air of refreshment upon them as if they had just had lunch' (*GE* 427).

But the character who is most profoundly and chronically divided is Pip; and perhaps the simplest and most effective means by which this division is registered is in the confusing effect it has upon the sensitive nature of Joe, who finds himself almost ridiculously appealing to the one who was ever the best of friends simultaneously as 'Pip' and 'Sir'. The irreversible effects of the split within the protagonist are made clear with great economy as Pip's accelerating recovery from his nervous breakdown brings with it a return on Joe's part to a recognition of the distance that has been set between them, expressed simply by his increasing use of the appelation 'Sir'.

The tremendous emotional cost of Pip's divided sensibility is measured against the much more pragmatic and negotiable version of it to be found in the lifestyle of Wemmick. A wholly farcical and pathetic parallel is also provided by the advancement of Wopsle, who follows Pip to London, similarly adopts a sophisticated-sounding foreign name (Waldengarver; Pip is nicknamed Handel), and attempts to act his way into a greater degree of fame and fortune. Like Pip, he has turned his back on a much more spiritually nourishing context for his endeavours – although this supposition depends on a little conventional symbolism, since, as far as Wopsle is concerned, even the Church ought to be open to competition – in order to devote himself to the pursuit of much more materialistic ambitions. Pip's great error is to opt for a context for his emotional life that he believes will refine the roughness he detects in himself, but where he actually finds himself is in a situation that is geared to enhance and exploit much worse forms of crudeness and insensitivity. He believes he is exchanging ignorance for knowledge, but one of the most shocking things he learns is that there is no essential difference between the rules of a society in which Pumblechook can succesfully pretend to be the maker of his fortune, and the rules that obtain in that wider world in which the real maker of his fortune turns out to be a convict. The farcical apparatus of Pumblechook's famously repeated insistence on shaking hands with the possessor of 'great expectations' – 'May I, May I?' – is precisely echoed in Magwitch's behaviour on his arrival in Pip's chambers, when he keeps on expressing his overwhelming desire to grasp Pip by the hands and just look at him.

In a ruthlessly logical fashion, the book keeps on demonstrating how Pip never in fact recovers from the moment when he was turned upside down over a gravestone in the church yard. It still seems to be happening to him on the day when he is made to realize his 'first decided experience of the stupendous power of money', when he is invited to dinner with Pumblechook and reports that 'if I had turned myself upside down before drinking, the wine could not have gone more direct to my head' (*GE* 180); and it happens again in a perhaps even more decided fashion on his twenty-first birthday, when he comes into his fortune and yet senses that 'I felt at a disadvantage, which reminded me of that old time when I had been put upon a tombstone' (*GE* 305). Pip never really sees things the right way up again; the text of *Great Expectations* supplies continual evidence of a situation in which one is in a sense always tilted backwards over a tombstone, held powerless in the grip of an oppressor, 'so that his eyes looked most powerfully down into mine, and mine looked most helplessly up into his' (*GE* 37). Here, right at the start of the text, the reader is provided with a model for the conditions of surveillance that prove to be fundamental to the economic basis of the society that *Great Expectations* discloses; it is a society in which the price paid or exacted for the pursuit of financial success necessitates exposure to inspection, of a kind that might have aggravated Dickens's own frustrations over being continually pressed for time in his role as a weekly serialist, and it may also throw some reflections on Dickens's childhood awareness of the demands made on him by a society in which his first experience of having to work for money involved him in the same nerve-wracking experience of being exposed to the public gaze.

7

Divided Selves

OUR MUTUAL FRIEND, A TALE OF TWO CITIES

About one-third of the way through *Our Mutual Friend* (1865), the character Mrs Wilfer is moved to pronounce on the impassable social distance that separates her and her family from another pair of characters, the Boffins. Her youngest daughter, Lavinia, or Lavvy, has just incited her sister Bella to what is adjudged to be an almost mutinous degree of 'levity', simply by asking her, 'And how are your Boffins?' Mrs Wilfer's reproach can stand as a fairly typical expression of the way she functions in the novel as a whole:

> 'this Lavinia, is my reason for objecting to a tone of levity. Mrs Boffin (of whose physiognomy I can never speak with the composure I would desire to preserve), and your mother, are not on terms of intimacy. It is not for a moment to be supposed that she and her husband dare to presume to speak of this family as the Wilfers. I cannot therefore condescend to speak of them as the Boffins. No; for such a tone – call it familiarity, levity, equality, or what you will – would imply those social interchanges which do not exist. Do I render myself intelligible?' (*OMF* 366)

It is possible to render Mrs Wilfer even more intelligible than she herself is aware by registering the presence of another phrase standing behind the one she actually employs:

> familiarity, levity, equality
> *fraternité, liberté, égalité*

The transformation of the phrase, not only in the context of this episode and of this strand of the novel, but also in the context of the novel as a whole, is particularly suggestive. It is also an example of something that is going on in Dickens all the time: the inability to let sleeping words lie, the need to reanimate dead bits of language, to resuscitate phrases that long usage has made almost meaningless. There are plenty of examples in this novel alone; and there are plenty of examples also in this novel of other tripartite phrases. Tripartite phrases seem to be designed to tie down words that will need redefinition in the course of the novel. One example comes from the end of the episode referred to above and is, quite simply, 'Our Mutual Friend', with each word emphasized by capitalization. Another is 'pounds, shillings and pence', which, by virtue of the formula L.s.d. gets translated into 'Luxury, Sensuality, Dissoluteness' – not a particularly subtle transformation, but its very lack of subtlety helps to make more obvious the impulse to transform.

Mrs Wilfer's special claim to the distortion of this catchword of the French Revolution stems from her abhorrence of vulgarity and her uninterrupted maintenance of an aristocratic hauteur, despite the fact that she has come from the lower middle class, has stayed in it by marrying Rumty, and is, to most intents and purposes, a virtual pauper. Despite her straitened circumstances, Mrs Wilfer's 'company manner' is nothing less than 'majestic': she conducts even the most trivial domestic business as if it were an affair of state and delivers judgement on the other members of her family in an 'Act of Parliament' tone. There is something almost admirable in this supreme indifference to financial status (in a society in which financial status is the only thing that counts), except that, of course, Mrs Wilfer's self-importance is related to her impecuniousness as a form of compensation for it. As a compensatory mechanism, it is, of course, an absurdity; not only in its deliberate obtuseness as to the all-importance of money, but also because it requires her to sustain a tone of gravity and of extreme formality even at the least appropriate moments, as when she 'abdicates' her 'culinary throne', but still proceeds to 'recommend examination of the bacon in the saucepan on the fire, and also of the potatoes by the application of a fork. Preparation of the greens will further become necessary if you persist in this unseemly demeanour' (*OMF* 447). Most of all, her simple plan to replace the importance of money with an assumption of breeding involves her in other kinds of imperceptiveness, specifically with regard to the characters of the Boffins, whom she farcically misjudges: 'Of the disinterestedness of their intentions towards Bella, I say nothing. But the craft, the secrecy, the dark deep underhanded plotting, written in Mrs Boffin's countenance, make me shudder' (*OMF* 117).

The ludicrous extremism of this recoil from those whom Mrs Wilfer considers to be vulgar, her distaste at the possibility of contamination by the undisguisably proletarian, is given a special flavour by a buried allusion to the French Revolution. Not only is she made to behave like an aristocrat; she is made to behave, in some obscure fashion, like a French aristocrat. And this supposition is reinforced by the picture she presents on the occasion of Bella's first 'interview' with the Boffins, when she sits stiffly by, 'like a functionary presiding over an interview previous to an execution' (*OMF* 113), as if Bella were about to be delivered up to the tumbrils of a howling revolutionary mob.

There is as a matter of fact one Frenchman actually present among the characters of *Our Mutual Friend*, the hapless visitor who is subjected to Podsnap's interrogatory techniques. The passage concerned seems mainly designed to give some measure of Podsnap's almost immeasurable self-conceit and chauvinism; but Podsnap is only a caricature of existing attitudes, and it seems significant that he should be brought to associate what is French with what is demotic – the French even speak, in certain respects, like the English lower classes: '"We call it Horse," said Mr Podsnap, with forbearance. "In England, Angleterre, England, We Aspirate the 'H', and We Say 'Horse'. Only our Lower Classes Say 'Orse!'."' (*OMF* 136) It is perhaps relevant to recall how much force this novel gives to questions of class in other, more apparently serious, contexts. All the characters are finely tuned to class distinctions and it is precisely a class barrier, real or feigned, that the two most important love relationships have to overcome. Moreover, the destructive power of class divisions is confirmed, in varying degrees, by the careers of characters such as Charley Hexam and Bradley Headstone.

The focus of the conversation between Podsnap and the Frenchman is ultimately more revealing. The question to which Mr Podsnap fails to elicit an answer is comically undermined and defused by the Frenchman's apparent incomprehension, although the fact that he is capable, once, at any rate, of a witty sally in English at least the equal of Podsnap's suggests that he is only stringing Podsnap along. But the question is a leading one: '"And Do You Find, Sir," pursued Mr Podsnap, with dignity, "Many Evidences that Strike You, of our British Constitution in the Streets Of The World's Metropolis, London, Londres, London?"' (*OMF* 136). The Frenchman does not answer, but the reader of the whole novel is well placed to answer, since many of the most important descriptive passages in *Our Mutual Friend* are given over to the establishment of just such a connection. Mr Podsnap would, perhaps, be gratified by thus much intelligence, though it is inconceivable that he would be gratified by the corollary of this observation – namely that the evidence to be seen in the streets is that the 'British Constitution' is rotten.

A little more than ten pages later comes one of the most celebrated evocations of the London street scene in the book, and what is striking about it, on the present reckoning, is that it draws a comparison between the English scene and the French, between London and Paris:

> That mysterious paper currency which circulates in London when the wind blows, gyrated here and there and everywhere. Whence can it come, whither can it go? It hangs on every bush, flutters in every tree, is caught flying by the electric wires, haunts every enclosure, drinks at every pump, cowers at every grating, shudders upon every plot of grass, seeks rest in vain behind the legions of iron rails. In Paris, where nothing is wasted, costly and luxurious city though it be, but where wonderful human ants creep out of holes and pick up every scrap, there is no such thing. There, it blows nothing but dust. There, sharp eyes and sharp stomachs reap even the east wind, and get something out of it. (*OMF* 147)

This is unmistakably something like an authorial answer to Podsnap's chauvinistically inspired question. And it is, just as unmistakably, a conceit: its elimination, at one stroke, of waste paper from the streets of Paris is hardly offered in the spirit of reportage. But the artificiality of the contrast does not necessarily damage it; Paris is not idealized – it is still a 'costly and luxurious' city, and numerous of its inhabitants have 'sharp eyes and sharp stomachs' – but, compared to London, the social and economic order it evinces is so much more efficient. It seems to Dickens to be somehow closer to a natural order of things, since even those in the most pinched of circumstances can 'reap' the east wind, and achieve something akin to the fabled purposefulness of the ant. In London, meanwhile, 'here and there and everywhere' is wastage: both material and human, as the anthropomorphism of the paper currency that 'haunts', 'drinks', 'cowers', 'shudders', and 'seeks rest in vain' makes clear. The common motion, nightmarishly circular, which constantly comes up against 'enclosures', 'gratings', and 'iron rails', is imprisoned within an order of meaningless repetitions, without reason or purpose: 'Whence can it come, whither can it go?' The systematic complexity of Dickens's writing in this novel is directed at just such an exploration of the ramifications of this situation as these questions require. The answer to the second question, 'whither can it go?', is obviously going to be less certain than the answer to the first. But it is remarkable that in this passage the alternative to the fruitlessness of London life should be so specific and so concrete; should be Paris.

The novel that explores these alternatives in greater detail and that questions the very nature of the relationship between alternatives is *A Tale of Two Cities* (1859), which begins famously by dividing its attention between 'the best of times' and 'the worst of times': 'it was the age of wisdom, it was the age of foolishness, it was the epoch of belief, it was the epoch of credulity', and so on (*TTC* 35). This generalization about the defining features of a historical period is based on the supposition that what appear to be mutually exclusive tendencies are actually complementary or even prone to be mistaken the one for the other. And this contradictoriness supplies the book with its most crucial means of organizing the plot and characterization.

Right from the start, it is the duplicity of appearances that is stressed, the debasement of face values. In the second chapter, the passengers on the Dover Mail are hidden, both physically and psychologically, from each other, and this circumstance not only allows Dickens to make revelations about their identities at a later stage in his plot; it also and more immediately engenders in the reader a sense of the impenetrability of other human beings. The text passes rapidly to narratorial comment on the closed nature of the 'book of life', which renders its messages illegible or inscrutable. Other peoples' lives remain essentially secret and mysterious. The men who travel with Mr Lorry in the coach are referred to as his 'fellow-inscrutables', and this nearly oxymoronic formulation, combining hints of both comradeship and reserve, is typical of the book's preference for narrative equivocation, for a potentially misleading caginess about the identities of those it is supposed to characterize.

Thematically, the novel is concerned with the hidden part of human lives, with what gets buried or submerged; and it is the attempt to disclose what has been sequestered that we see exemplified in Lorry's mission to dig Manette out of the grave of his prison existence, to recall him to life; as also in Carton's desire to dig down and recover a former potential from the desert his own life has become. These processes of excavation that carry overtones of spiritual renewal are of course parodied by Jerry Cruncher's activities as a grave-robber; the manic impiety of this resurrectionist is carefully revoked at the end with Carton's cherishing the memory of his father's funeral with the intoning of the service, 'I am the Resurrection and the Life...', and so on. Equally important are the institutional parallels in the emphasis on suppression and incarceration. The buried life in the Bastille is counterpointed by the 'underground secrets' of Tellson's bank, with its heavy iron bars, restriction of movement, and sense of claustrophobia; the bank even has a 'Condemned Hold'.

Mr Lorry himself is divided in two in a way that involves the suppression and censorship of certain aspects of his personality; he becomes shrewdly businesslike in the bank, but emotionally embattled out of it, protesting vainly that 'I have no feelings; I am a mere machine' (*TTC* 54). But this kind of conflict, which is largely a source of humour in connection with Lorry, also generates possibilities of melodrama, sentimentality, and even of cultural critique, elsewhere. The most obvious complementarity in the book is that between the physically similar Charles Darnay and Sydney Carton. But there is also the doubling of roles in the twin-brother relationship of Charles's father and uncle; in the employment of disguise that makes Solomon Pross and John Barsad the same man; in the duplication that makes young Jerry a miniature version of his father; and in Lucy's capacity to be two people in one, to appear to her rediscovered father to be both her own mother and herself, putting him in mind not only of the family and home that 'once were', but also of the family and home that will be in the future. It is a meditation on the divergence between actuality and potential that dominates the waking life of Sydney Carton, who constantly compares himself with Darnay: 'he shows you [he says to himself] what you have fallen away from, and what you might have been!' (*TTC* 116). These are only the major instances of a textual effect, sometimes strenuously insisted on, sometimes only casually alluded to, in which people, settings, situations, and events promise to be more than one thing; often, precisely two things at one and the same time.

But is there anything of real significance that interrupts this catalogue or record of scissions and rivalries, doublings and divisions? Is there anything important in the organization of the text that does not undergo the usual kind of fission and which resists a fascination with the ambivalent? If anything, it is the Revolution itself, which is, in formal terms at least, integral and unitary. The catchphrase that most effectively renders the structure of ideas and feelings of the time in a form of language is 'The Republic *One and Indivisible*, of Liberty, Equality, Fraternity, or Death!' (*TTC* 275; emphases added). A corollary of this idea of indivisibility is found perhaps rather surprisingly in the description of the action of the mob, which has the indivisibility of a sea, of a surging mass, a composite form in which individual purposes are submerged, and submitted to the united current, which sweeps up everyone alike.

In *A Tale of Two Cities* the sense of a gap between inner and outer, between a buried life and the social veneer, is historically urgent, because it informs a British society that has not even had the chance to learn from mistakes, as the French can claim they have, or as Dickens can claim for them. And this is why, in its ending, the novel indulges in a romance of completion, of the repairing of fractured identities, the resolving of ambiguities, the eradication of divisions, which it is otherwise so concerned to preserve and trace.

In *Our Mutual Friend* the importance of a veneer, of an outer crust that belies, to a greater or lesser degree, whatever it covers over or supplants, leads inevitably to an almost universal practice of role playing. A theatrical lexicon of prompts, cues, learning the lines or learning the book, walking onstage and walking offstage, is used with a remarkable assiduity, most unignorably in the cases of the Lammles and Fledgeby. The Lammles, who have cheated each other into marriage on false pretences – so successful are the appearances they present to the world – are forced to play their parts as satisfied husband and wife in order to be able to cheat others, while Fledgeby press-gangs the kindly Riah into a form of play-acting that will further his own extortionate schemes. Eugene, before his involvement with Lizzie becomes wholly disinterested, is prone to dissimulations; so that once his 'part is played out for the evening' he can 'come off stage' (*OMF* 400). Boffin, of course, has to act the part of miser, while John Rokesmith acts the part of himself. Wegg and, for a certain time, Venus have to put on a performance repeatedly in order to belie the true nature of their interest in Boffin and the mounds. Meanwhile Bradley Headstone tries desperately and fails to act the part of schoolmaster, which represents the only means within his reach of achieving the social status he craves; when he assumes the costume of Rogue Riderhood, it seems less of an act than his usual assumption of a schoolmaster's role: 'whereas, in his own schoolmaster clothes, he usually looked as if they were the clothes of some other man, he now looked, in the clothes of some other man or men, as if they were his own' (*OMF* 619).

The torturing division within Bradley Headstone is perhaps the cruellest instance of a process by which the exigency of acting a part ultimately produces a doubleness of self. There are intimations of the same process being well advanced in Headstone's pupil, Charlie Hexam: 'There was a curious mixture in the boy, of uncompleted savagery, and uncompleted civilization' (*OMF* 28). Bella protests that her life and fortunes are 'contradictory' and is restlessly aware of her damaging condition as a 'doubly spoilt girl; spoilt first by poverty, and then by wealth' (*OMF* 305). John Harmon, who returns to England 'divided in my mind' (*OMF* 360), is faced with the prospect either of acting a part already prepared for him, with all the lines, as it were, already written out, or of acting the part of his natural self, with a script of his own devising. His only method of preserving a sense of integrity is by opting to pose as the double of himself. The chapter in which he debates the dilemma is entitled 'A Solo and A Duett'. Among the other most important male characters, those who are not split in two themselves appear as separated halves requiring to be joined in a pair in order to be able to function. Eugene and Mortimer are such, Mortimer being described as 'but the double of the friend on whom he has founded himself' (*OMF* 404). Their surnames would seem to bear out an interdependence, 'Lightwood' being required as tinder in order to be able to make the 'Wray-burn'. Wegg, who is so far gone in duplicity that 'he ranged with that very numerous class of impostors, who are quite as determined to keep up appearances to themselves, as to their neighbours' (*OMF* 61), attempts to recruit Venus as the only man he is able to call his 'Twin', although Venus's eventual dissociation from Wegg is one of the triumphs in the book of a personal recovery of integrity. Wegg's misjudgement of Boffin centres on the apprehension of his employer's 'double look', although Boffin proves to be as singular and straightforward as Venus surmises, uncorrupted despite his custody of the Harmon fortune, the perverted legacy of a man whose own divided nature is revealed in his provision of more than one will. The antithetical state of singularity is typically embodied in Betty Higden; indeed, she is a paragon of not wanting to 'set up a contradiction' within herself, stating a clear ambition of continuing 'to be of a piece like, and helpful of myself right through to my death' (*OMF* 377).

Survival in the world of *Our Mutual Friend* requires a falsification of the self, identification with the social role one is expected to play, whose chronic and radical effects may include a disabling and even catastrophic fission of self in which it is precisely the instinctual life and moral awareness that decline towards extinction.

The streets are full of extinction – of physical detritus comprised of dust, paper, pins, grit, and the desiccated remains of fallen leaves. It never disappears; all through the novel it can be found pervading or seeking its way into hair, clothes, eyes, ears, mouth, nose, even skin, so that even living beings are instinct with dead matter. In Paris it can somehow, mysteriously, be reaped; but in London it is the irreducibly sterile end product of wasted efforts, of uselessly spent energies, the subtle and oppressive residue of dead lives. When it is accumulated into great heaps and mounds in the yard of Harmony Jail, its sheer physical presence and the dead weight it imposes, metaphorically speaking, on the lives of those who, in a different order of things, would stand to benefit from it as a potential source of wealth, express the colossal wastage in human and material terms of an entire social and economic order whose highest legislative and administrative procedures are rendered by precisely the same means:

> My lords and gentlemen and honourable boards, when you in the course of your dust-shovelling and cinder-raking have piled up a mountain of pretentious failure, you must off with your honourable coats for the removal of it, and fall to the work with the power of all the queen's horses and all the queen's men, or it will come rushing down and bury us alive. (*OMF* 495–6)

The self-interest that leads in the extremest cases to hoarding of the sort that results in the Harmon mounds, produces inefficiencies and inequalities in the system of exchanges that transform the gigantic reserves of human purposefulness into sheer waste or misuse. It is not until Boffin starts to remove the mountains of pretentious failure from the yard of Harmony Jail that Harmon's fortune once again begins to sparkle, 'after a long long rust in the dark', and this is only possible because Bella has been partially educated out of the state in which she calls herself 'the most mercenary little wretch that ever lived in the world', in order to become 'the true golden gold at heart' (*OMF* 752). Jenny Wren, meanwhile, provides a continuous example of the possibility of turning dust into gold in her capacity for producing masterpieces of the doll's dressmaker's art out of 'damage and waste', so that Riah is able to observe, 'Our waste goes into the best of company' (*OMF* 278). Her powers of transformation are, of course, identified with her imaginative transcendence of this city of black shades, her ability to 'come up and be dead' (*OMF* 280).

Despite Wegg's protestations to Venus that 'You can't buy human flesh and blood in this country, sir; not alive, you can't' (*OMF* 295), the fact is that human beings in the society of *Our Mutual Friend* are reducible to units of exchange. An endless supply of equally dispensable human units is what is uncovered by the Boffins' search for an orphan to adopt. They soon have to thread their way through a minefield of 'genuine' and 'counterfeit' 'orphan-stock' and orphan 'scrip', perplexed by the fluctuations of a 'rigged' market in which an orphan might be at 5,000 per cent discount in the morning and then at 5,000 per cent premium by noon (*OMF* 195). Elsewhere, Dickens makes a point, in the most effectively schematic way, about the loss in terms of individual differentiation that is involved when the application of the principles of bargain and sale across the whole range of human activities works to eclipse the history that would otherwise have been the detailed and congested record of a highly specific adult life. He does this in the famous passage that revolves around the reiteration of the word 'shares'. The passage comprises a series of questions with corresponding answers. The questions if answered properly would go to make up the outline of a uniquely determined life, providing information about background and motivations, but each of the various questions is met with the same monotonous answer: 'Where does he come from? Shares. Where is he going to? Shares' (*OMF* 118). A specific human complexity is reduced to the level of the lowest common denominator – exchange value – which is the only thing the character recognizes in himself and others, or is recognized for. The totalizing scope of this systematic erosion of individual differences is felt even in contexts of the most casual and least apparently cost-effective of human transactions, so that even gossip – for example, on the subject of what is called the Harmon Murder – is something that one may want to have 'a share in', an interest in which makes one a 'part proprietor'. Even Sloppy, who would prefer his work to be rewarded not with money but with a song, cannot altogether escape the attempts to engross him in a world that will automatically translate his physical ineptness and general appearance of being a misfit into a form of social insolvency: 'A considerable capital of knee and elbow and wrist and ankle, had Sloppy, and he didn't know how to dispose of it to the best advantage, but was always investing it in wrong securities, and so getting himself into embarrassed circumstances' (*OMF* 201).

Irrespective of the value invested in it or denied it, the social self is disposed of by others, manipulable like household articles, when it is not in a position to inflict such a status on others. And so Bella, who has been disposed of in Harmon's will, suffers the indignity of being treated like a 'dozen of spoons', and Miss Podsnap, 'or any other young person properly born and bred', according to Podsnap himself, is liable to be 'put away like the plate, brought out like the plate, polished like the plate, counted, weighed, and valued like the plate' (*OMF* 146). The repeated insistence on the grounds of the simile might have the paradoxical effect of raising doubts about its viability. But the simile is only a convenience, and it is swept aside in Mr Milvey's conception of the chain of substitutions that sets a tariff against the disposable orphans: 'even if you exchanged blankets for the child,' he warns, '– or books and firing – it would be impossible to prevent their being turned into liquor' (*OMF* 110).

To the extent that characters cannot identify, or are unhappy at the prospect of identifying, with the social roles they are expected to play, they are made to realize the extent to which they exist merely as the property of strangers. Wegg is the most spectacular, and farcical, example of man as object, man as the property of strangers. He is, in fact, with his wooden leg, part man and part object, exhibiting in his own anatomy the concrete realization of an everywhere abstract process of reification. And the continued and separate existence of his missing leg in Venus's collection of 'human warious' dramatizes the alienating effect of being at the disposal of others, allowed a status and a presence only as an object, which is interchangeable with other and equivalent objects. The summit of Wegg's ambitions is to reintegrate himself by coming into the possession of all the separate parts of himself, by buying himself back, as it were:

> 'I have a prospect of getting on in life and elevating myself by my own independent exertions,' says Wegg, feelingly, 'and I shouldn't like – I tell you openly I should *not* like – under such circumstances, to be what I may call dispersed, a part of me here, and a part of me there, but should wish to collect myself like a genteel person.' (*OMF* 88)

Wegg's present condition of doubleness could never be repaired and transformed into a true singleness, as his fatal aspirations to gentility make clear; what he has in mind by collecting himself into one is the assumption of an image of uniformity that a social role would endow him with and which others could recognize and act up to.

His physical incompleteness is a literalized version of the partial existences endured by nearly all the characters in the novel. Very often they are introduced as shadows of their potential selves, brought into focus anonymously, with the relevant visual information withheld, as if they were announcing, as Rokesmith explicitly does announce, 'I am nobody... and not likely to be known' (*OMF* 99). Rokesmith retains his aura of indefiniteness for very obvious reasons, his face overshadowed by a 'nameless' cloud, and his movements in the Wilfer household as elusive as a ghost's. But his initial appearance as only a part of himself, a disembodied face in a doorway, is duplicated with the emergence of several other characters in the narrative. Riderhood materializes suddenly in the doorway of Lightwood's office as no more and no less than 'a something in the likeness of a man' (*OMF* 150). Venus is introduced as a face, around which his character is gradually composed in a faltering process of deduction which rests on negative proofs: 'His eyes are like the over-tried eyes of an engraver, but he is not that; his expression and stoop are like those of a shoemaker, but he is not that' (*OMF* 83). When Mrs Boffin is unsettled in her attempt to displace the effects of the past by wishful thinking about the future, she is disturbed by the sensation of a 'face growing out of the dark'; 'Noddy' she says, 'the faces of the old man and the two children are all over the house tonight' (*OMF* 190). Most of all, the severely repressed personality of Bradley Headstone becomes increasingly subject to such wholly irreconcilable impulses that it is almost as if his head becomes completely detached from his body, and pursues its task of keeping track of Eugene's movements almost independently: 'he went by them in the dark, like a haggard head suspended in the air: so completely did the force of his expression cancel his figure' (*OMF* 534).

The most easily identifiable constraints on the lives of the characters, both in the primary plot centred on the denizens of Harmony Jail and in the ancillary plot concerned with the Lammles and the Veneering circle, take their course within the limits prescribed by legal documents: by the marriage contract that the Lammles convert into a business arrangement, the charter of their 'mutual understanding' that they will exploit the misplaced trust of others for their own financial advantage; and the contractual basis of the will by means of which the dead Harmon binds his surviving legatees to a choice of cruel alternatives, which is no real choice at all. The legalized demoralization that is the sequel to these arrangements finds a clear echo in the inequities of the social contract as a whole; the most tendentious writing in the book is diametrically opposed to the scandalous claims of Podsnap that 'there is not a country in the world where so noble a provision is made for the poor as in this country' (*OMF* 143).

The most signal aspect of any life lived under the conditions of one of these contracts is a dismaying loss of initiative. Bella and John Harmon have their options severely limited; the most decisive turning points in their lives have already been decided. The unnaturalness of this situation is brought home by the authorship of an alternative will, that of the orphan Johnny, whose kiss bequeathed to the 'boofer lady' is meant to be conveyed to Bella by Harmon in the person of Rokesmith, and thus entails bringing them together on the wholly different basis of spontaneous affection. But even after Rokesmith has conceived enough of a passion for Bella to want to propose to her, he still feels compelled to enter his plea as if it were a legal application, and Bella responds in kind, as if the subtext to their declarations was a consciousness of the need to renegotiate their legal positions. It is only when their relationship is sustained by an unforced and mutual regard that Bella is able to emerge from a mentality in which the future can be conceived of only as something dictated in advance; she maps out her coming life only insofar as this can be done in a game of fortune telling, which involves guesswork and a process of divination with intimations of spiritual guidance – an altogether chancy procedure wholly divorced from the unshakeable fixities of a will.

In equivalent ways, the lives of Mortimer and Eugene are intended to follow the patterns laid down for them by respective parents:

> 'It was forced upon me,' said the gloomy Eugene, 'because it was understood that we wanted a barrister in the family. We have got a precious one.'
>
> 'It was forced upon me,' said Mortimer, 'because it was understood that we wanted a solicitor in the family. And we have got a precious one.' (*OMF* 29)

Eugene and Mortimer at least have the intellectual resources – and the economic resources – to be able to develop a cynical detachment. In a differently placed character like Mr Dolls, the attempt to struggle against 'circumstances over which had no control' (*OMF* 241) ends in appalling disorientation. Mr Dolls's catchphrase is also employed by Rumty, who similarly abnegates his responsibilities in a reversal of the terms of his relationship with his own child. All these characters are, in one sense or another, imprisoned by the consciousness of structures intended to fit over their lives and confine their scope. The emotional confinement in which Bella and John Harmon are expected to live is a part of the project devised by a man who is more than once referred to as 'the dead Jailer of Harmony Jail' (*OMF* 106).

The wholly foreseeable result of such restrictions in a character like Eugene is a chronic lassitude, an aimlessness, an undirectedness, a consistency only in a 'susceptibility to boredom' (*OMF* 150). Eugene feels his life to be unlivable in any meaningful terms; he is unable to answer Mortimer's questions, 'What is to come of it? What are you doing? Where are you going?' (*OMF* 293) – another of the book's organizing interrogations – and pronounces himself 'ridiculous', just as Bella pronounces herself 'ridiculous'. His relation to the very idea of energy – which he is ultimately to embody, as a 'mine of purpose and energy' (*OMF* 735), once he has been galvanized by his love for Lizzie – is initially so remote that he cannot realize it as anything more than a word: 'If there is a word in the dictionary under any letter from A to Z that I abominate, it is energy' (*OMF* 29–30).

Eugene's apathy and powerlessness are counterpointed by, and even actually pitted against, the fanatical intensity of Bradley Headstone. Their behaviour in the streets is tellingly contradistinctive: Headstone 'lurks' while Eugene 'loiters'. Bradley is someone who has imposed an artificial structure on his own life that virtually kills him by the effort required to keep it in place and make it work. His chosen profession of schoolmaster offers him the only means of establishing himself in a society that has no use for, or tolerance of, his ferocious instinctual drives, and the result is a sundering of his nature into two halves that informs his every movement with an unbearable nervous tension. The fact that he is a schoolmaster ties him directly to the same social contract that translates every form of endeavour into monetary terms, because his system of learning is a process of 'mechanical stowage' that piles up knowledge in a 'wholesale warehouse'. Knowledge is accumulated like stock; it is Bradley's investment in society; it is amassed and hoarded like the mounds of dead matter in the yard of Harmony Jail. It is a sheer dead weight of facts, painstakingly acquired through a system of rote learning that totally ignores the education of character and that is announced by the droning of schoolchildren that prepares for the first appearance of Bradley in the text. He is introduced not even as a face but as a disembodied intoning voice, and, when his physical appearance is given, it is dominated by a 'want of adaption' between him and his clothes, suggesting that he is only acting a role in which nothing quite fits. He is a miser of knowledge who 'clutches' hold of his facts, reproducing the jealous and suspicious motions of old Harmon that have even been transmitted into the 'tight-clenched' furniture of Harmony Jail. The crushing and constricting effects of this education are paralleled in the workings of what is called 'the faith and school of Podsnappery', whose curriculum for the day includes a variety of pursuits and disciplines, Arts and Sciences, which all, nevertheless, express only one thing: they are 'respectfully descriptive of getting up at eight, shaving close at a quarter past, breakfasting at nine, going to the City at ten, coming home at half-past five, and dining at seven' (*OMF* 132). Just as everything you ever need to know about any man is only one thing: shares. For as long as Eugene conducts his relationship with Lizzie in terms of wanting to educate her, the reader remains suspicious, since the kind of education he has in mind is for the sole purpose of raising her above her own class and making her 'fit in'.

Bradley Headstone's characteristic activities of 'lurking' and 'clutching' are constantly echoed in the behaviour, respectively, of the various characters referred to as one or another kind of 'bird of prey', and of misers (real, like Old Harmon; or feigned, like Boffin), and especially of Wegg and Venus in the period of their association. Betty Higden's great fear is of being 'clutched off' to a 'great blank barren Union House' (*OMF* 498). The amount of nervous strain involved in having constantly to 'lurk' and 'clutch' in order to function in this world of misers and predators takes its most obvious toll in the case of Headstone, who becomes more and more physically haggard and prone to sudden great spurts of blood from the nose. On the occasion of his lying in wait for Lizzie, 'lurking at a corner', he can be seen working at a gravestone with his fingers, rubbing it into powder, which seems symbolic of his auto-destructive urges, given the associative link made possible by his name: Headstone.

Headstone is destroyed from within, by the furnace of animal passions that he has provided no outlet for, that he has repressed, clamped down for so long and with such undue severity that the only possible outcome of the immense build-up of pressure entailed is a paroxysm of murderous rage. Of course, his humble origins mean that he is hardly likely to be able to resist the temptation of advancement held out to him by the particular social role he sets himself so laboriously to acquire, unlike Eugene, who is initially vacuous and insipid precisely because he can afford to be. But the imagery of destruction by fire is peculiar to Headstone, and elsewhere fire is allowed the function of engendering warmth, as in the case of Lizzie, and of Wrayburn, with his appropriate name. Lizzie's sympathetic powers seem intimately linked to her gazing at the 'hollow down by the flare' (*OMF* 77). This doubleness of function is extended to all the elemental presences in the book – including the river. The river is an enveloper of corrupted lives and a disgorger of corpses, but it is also intended to mark that stage in the passage of a character's life when he is ready to 'come up and be dead' in the sense that he has ceased to 'look alive' in the terms that Fledgeby would employ. It sets a seal on the renovation of a character who has found some means of reconciling himself to his affective life, just as it equally consumes and extinguishes all those who have wasted their capacity for an affective life. It comes to be associated with the regeneration of Harmon and Wrayburn, but can also be used to indicate the seething and sliding depths in Headstone's make-up; it can be made to suggest how he is fated to be at one with the slime and ooze of the river bed.

A relationship with natural forces is directly negotiated with the agency of the sympathetic imagination, whose constant guardians are Lizzie and the extraordinary Jenny, who carries around a version of harmonized nature in her own person – the 'bower' of her golden hair – and whose rooftop garden among the scudding clouds and winds is the setting for a redefinition of the categories of life and death. But there is also Venus, the figure Dickens felt impelled to include in his novel after discovering a real-life counterpart. Venus, as his name suggests he ought to be, is motivated chiefly by love, and is one of those figures in the novel who is capable of turning waste into gold; he is an articulator of skeletons, a reintegrator of scattered parts, unlike Wegg, the fraudulent poetaster, who disarticulates language, both in his own compositions and in his readings of Gibbon, which mangle the latter's periodic prose, dispersing its meanings haphazardly. Venus almost seems able to bring the dead to life, since many of the items in his collection of 'human warious' – the Frenchman, the Hindoo baby, the Alligator, for example – seem much more animated than many of the inhabitants of the streets. Venus is the flawed but patient craftsman who, in an almost lunatic fashion, seems able to produce the illusion that it is possible to reverse the processes at work in the society that surrounds him. In the large and small structures of this novel, Dickens is doing something that resembles this. Looking hard enough at any phrase always implies another one (*fraternité, liberté, égalité*), just as looking hard enough and close enough at any given form of society always suggests an alternative; London implies Paris. Understanding the conditions in which everyone feels like the property of strangers leads to the possibility of imagining a world composed entirely of mutual friends.

8

Concluding

'DR MARIGOLD'S PRESCRIPTIONS', *THE MYSTERY OF EDWIN DROOD*

In 1858 Dickens commenced a series of public readings for his own benefit. This commercializing of an activity he had previously carried on for charitable purposes sharpened his perception of himself as an artist exposed more conspicuously than most to the gaze of the public. An enhanced sense of being at work in the 'shop window' is testified to with considerable bravado in the short text 'Dr Marigold's Prescriptions'. This monologue was written in 1865 specifically for public performance. Its first-person protagonist is a 'cheap jack', an auctioneer of trashy, second-hand goods who operates out of the back of a cart; like Dickens himself, especially when onstage, he is entirely dependent on the success of his 'patter' to earn a living. The subject matter consists of accounts of the pathetic death of his daughter and of the derangement and death of his wife, which is followed by his adoption of another daughter, whom he brings up and eventually marries off. It is a sequence of events that follows a pattern fundamental to many of Dickens's narratives: the catastrophic demise of a 'natural' family is succeeded by the reparative, restorative experience of creating an adoptive one. What is unusual about this version of the predicament is the way in which the language of personal affection, of emotional values, is actually filtered through the economic opportunism of a monologist who depends on his verbal abilities to earn a living:

> 'Now, you country boobies,' says I, *feeling as if my heart was a heavy weight at the end of a broken sash-line*, 'now let's know what you want to-night, and you shall have it. But first of all, shall I tell you why I

have got this little girl round my neck? You don't want to know? Then you shall. She belongs to the Fairies. She is a fortune-teller. She can tell me all about you in a whisper, and can put me up to whether you're a going to buy a lot or leave it. Now do you want a saw? No, she says you don't, because you're too clumsy to use one. Your well-known awkwardness would make it manslaughter. Now I am a going to ask her what you do want. *(Then I whispered, 'Your head burns so, that I am afraid it hurts you bad, my pet?' and she answered, without opening her heavy eyes, 'Just a little, father.')* Oh! This little fortune-teller says it's a memorandum-book you want. Then why didn't you mention it? Here it is. Look at it. Two hundred superfine hot-pressed wire-wove pages, ready ruled for your expenses, an everlastingly-pointed pencil to put 'em down with, a double-bladed penknife to scratch 'em out with, a book of printed tables to calculate your income with, and a camp-stool to sit down upon while you give your mind to it! Stop! And an umbrella to keep the moon off when you give your mind to it on a pitch dark night. Now I won't ask you how much for the lot, but how little? How little are you thinking of? Don't be ashamed to mention it, because my fortune-teller knows already. *(Then making believe to whisper, I kissed her, and she kissed me.)* Why, she says you are thinking of as little as three and threepence! I couldn't have believed it, even of you, unless she told me. Three and threepence! And a set of printed tables in the lot that'll calculate your income up to forty thousand a year, you grudge three and sixpence. Well then, I'll tell you my opinion. I so despise the threepence, that I'd sooner take three shillings. There. For three shillings, three shillings, three shillings! Gone. Hand 'em over to the lucky man.'

As there had been no bid at all, everybody looked about and grinned at everybody, while I touched little Sophy's face and asked her if she felt faint or giddy. 'Not very, father. It will soon be over.' Then turning from the pretty patient eyes, which were opened now, and seeing nothing but grins across my lighted grease-pot, I went on again in my Cheap Jack style. 'Where's the butcher?' *(My sorrowful eye had just caught sight of a fat young butcher on the outside of the crowd.)* 'She says the good luck is the butcher's. Where is he?' Everybody handed on the blushing butcher to the front, and there was a roar, and the butcher felt himself obliged to put his hand in his pocket and take the lot. The party so picked out, in general does feel obliged to take the lot. Then we had another lot the counterpart of that one, and sold it sixpence cheaper, which is always wery much enjoyed. So I went on in my Cheap Jack style till we had the ladies' lot – the tea-pot, tea-caddy, glass sugar basin, half a dozen spoons, and caudle-cup – *and all the time I was making similar excuses to give a look or two and say a word or two to my poor child. It was while the second ladies' lot was holding 'em enchained that I felt her lift herself a little on my shoulder, to*

> *look across the dark street. 'What troubles you, darling?' 'Nothing troubles me, father. I am not at all troubled. But don't I see a pretty churchyard over there?' 'Yes, my dear.' 'Kiss me twice, dear father, and lay me down to rest upon that churchyard grass so soft and green.'* I staggers back into the cart with her head dropped on my shoulder, and I says to her mother, 'Quick. Shut the door! Don't let those laughing people see!' 'What's the matter?' she cries. 'O, woman, woman,' I tells her, 'you'll never catch my little Sophy by her hair again, for she's dead and flown away from you!' (*SN* 214–15)

The most intimate details of Marigold's tragic personal life have to be exploited or at the least made to coincide with the exigencies of his financial situation. The stress on the item of the memorandum-book is particularly revealing. This book, or one very like it, recurs in the relationship he develops with his adoptive daughter, also called Sophy. Intriguingly, the second Sophy is deaf and dumb. Not blind; although she resembles the figures of Laura Bridgeman and Oliver Caswell in *American Notes for General Circulation*, in being exempt from the generally prevailing conditions of amenability to control. She cannot hear Marigold's patter, and does not operate in terms of a deceitful language that is dominated by survival tactics and prompted by the 'stupendous power of money'. The second Sophy stands for a radical innocence and an essential privacy; except that, while the language of emotion and affection remains intact in her exchanges, it is also curiously magnified. When she strikes up a relationship with another deaf-mute, a young man who becomes her lover, the necessity to sign their most intimate messages makes their emotional life totally readable to the cheap-jack: 'At last I was by accident present at a meeting between them in the open air, looking on, leaning behind a fir-tree without their knowing of it. It was a moving meeting for all the three parties concerned. I knew every syllable that passed between them as well as they did' (*SN* 224). Paradoxically, the couple whose language can hide nothing, have nothing to hide.

The cheap-jack, in creating a new family, also creates a new language; when she is still very young, he begins the task of teaching Sophy how to communicate using a primal language that simply gives names to things: 'cart' is inscribed on the side of the cart; 'Doctor Marigold' is the legend that he hangs around his own neck. It is an Edenic language that predates deception, treachery, linguistic corruption, but it is also one that can be maintained only in an intensely private context.

After he has taught Sophy the rudiments of communication, he leaves her, regretfully, at a Deaf and Dumb Establishment in London. For two years, he prepares for her graduation and return by assembling a library for her use and then by compiling a book for her entertainment, 'Doctor Marigold's Prescriptions'. This is a book of which there is only one copy, and for which there will be only one reader. The private circuit of meaning it creates can be seen as a redemption of Dickens's own situation, in which financial imperatives drove him towards mass-production and an unimaginably large audience.

Despite his being a novelist very obviously in the market place, Dickens's ambition was to maintain somehow, in his own mind at least, a close relationship with his readers. In the speech he made on the first occasion of his reading for profit, he registers both the distance that has been set up between himself and his readers, and his need to cross that distance. Public reading, he says, is 'a tried means of strengthening those relations – I may almost say of personal friendship – which it is my great privilege and pride, as it is my great responsibility, to hold with a multitude of persons who will never hear my voice nor see my face!' (*S*. 264).

Sophy, like so many of Dickens's characters, whether in his fiction or in the scheme of Urania Cottage, is made to emigrate – this time to China – in order to start life anew, beyond the social contract of nineteenth-century Britain. She returns, only at the very end of the monologue, in order to present Marigold with her own daughter, the replica, but significantly a speaking replica, of herself, the gift of speech representing a last-minute, impossible projection, the willing into being of an intensely private, uninvaded individual, who for once is not maimed or disabled in any way.

In many ways, 'Dr Marigold's Prescriptions' achieves a conspectus of lifelong Dickensian preoccupations, while *The Mystery of Edwin Drood* would seem to be striking out in a quite new direction – although it is risky trying to make good such a claim when dealing with an unfinished novel. The texture and tone of *Drood* are unlike any other of Dickens's works; the humour is seldom vivacious, and is even somewhat jaded. There is very little indication of authorial sentiment, and a more pervasive sense of disillusionment with human relations. There is a strict organization of thematic elements, although the motivation behind specific themes is sometimes unclear. The incompleteness of the plot invites two kinds of critical response: speculation about the unfolding of the mystery, and a contrasting emphasis on characterization and rhetorical structure. There is no shortage of critical experiments in the first of these two veins, and I intend to concentrate on the second.

The most remarkable character in *Drood,* John Jasper, becomes the centre of attention for all the others, who attempt to read the meaning of his behaviour as avidly as any of the novel's critics. The intensity of his passion for Rosa Bud is reminiscent of Bradley Headstone's attachment to Lizzie Hexam, except that the outrageous proposal of marriage he makes in Miss Twinkleton's garden is a more graphically uncompromising verbal assault than anything Headstone manages. What is astonishing about this speech is that it is less a declaration of love than the revelation of a desire for hate. Jasper's behaviour is governed by a fantasy of being rejected by Rosa; not once, but over and over again: 'I don't ask you for your love; give me yourself and your hatred; give me yourself and that pretty rage; give me yourself and that enchanting scorn; it will be enough for me' (*MED* 229). The slightly varied repetitiveness of these and other invitations give Jasper's speech a pornographic single-mindedness. The masochistic violence of his imagination is anaesthetized by opium; but the degradation of the opium den allows him to despise himself and justify the contempt of others.

Headstone's moral inferiority is accentuated by contrast with the respectability of his profession of schoolmaster. The discrepancy between public office and hidden depravity is much more glaring in the case of Jasper, who has to perform the role of cathedral functionary while cultivating his secret vice and nursing his murderous passion. But his mesmerizing effect on readers, both in the story and of the story, should not distract attention away from the extent to which other characters are subject to impulses towards masochism.

Grewgious has spent his life in the aftermath of rejection by Rosa's mother (a rejection assured by his never giving her the chance to accept him) and binding himself to carry out the wishes of his rival. Durdles employs Deputy to stone him from the churchyard whenever the latter catches him still out of doors after ten o' clock; Durdles shows more interest in being stoned than in avoiding the risk of injury. The spectacle of his being scapegoated in this manner (a condition reflected in Deputy's laming a sheep) arouses a ferocious response in Jasper. Crisparkle mortifies the flesh by diving several times into the icy Cloisterham Weir in December weather; his pretext is a search for Edwin Drood's belongings, but his immersion recalls the episode of his near-drowning in youth, a trauma that he forces himself repeatedly to encounter. All these men are bachelors whose closest relationship is with subordinates they themselves are submissive to: Grewgious maintains the fantasy of inferiority to his own clerk, Bazzard; Durdles submits to the energetic verbal and physical abuse of a working-class boy; while Crisparkle is devoted to his pupil Neville Landless, despite, or perhaps because of, the reputation for physical violence he acquires. All of them have avoided the development of a relationship with a member of the opposite sex that would test their masculinity by conventional means. The most impressive example of masculinity is Tartar, who has proved his mettle in an act of homosocial bonding by saving the youthful Crisparkle from drowning. Crisparkle's subsequent prowess at swimming commemorates that bond and allows him to embody masculinity himself. The death by drowning of Rosa's mother implicates her surviving suitors in a silent admission of sexual inadequacy. The possibility that Edwin has perished by drowning follows his own misgivings on the subject of his own manliness. Rosa has clearly found a substitute for him in the physically resourceful Tartar, a sailor whose deftness with the rowing boat is set off by Grewgious's incompetence. The wide experience of the much-travelled Tartar is seen to best advantage when contrasted with the spurious cosmopolitanism of Sapsea: 'If I have not gone to foreign countries, young man, foreign countries have come to me' (*MED* 64). Even Mr Sapsea's name suggests oxymoronically a close confinement of the masculine tendency to adventure.

Dickens arranges a powerful hint that Edwin has actually been immured in one of the vaults of the cathedral, where his remains have been disposed of by quicklime. But the idea of drowning has more importance in the rhetorical structure of the text. To drown is to fail to take part in the imperial adventure, in the experience of overseas. Contact with foreigners sharpens the sense of what is English and what is manly, and confirms the significance of the equation between the two. *The Mystery of Edwin Drood* is a novel in which foreign countries come to Cloisterham: Chinese selling opium, the Landless siblings with their 'dark blood', the entire contents of Tartar's room.

In many ways, the most remarkable aspect of the novel is the susceptibility of Rosa Bud to the foreign and the degenerate. She is attracted first of all to the mixed blood of Neville Landless, and then to a man whose name, Tartar, holds out an ambiguous promise of the East. Rosa has a weakness for Turkish sweetmeats, referred to rather oddly as 'Lumps-of Delight', a phrase that suggests the basic materials for Jasper's more serious addiction to opium. Above all, Rosa herself embodies a fundamentally mixed nature, a mixture of feelings, of both fascination and repulsion, for the figure of Jasper, whose name is a word of oriental origin for a stone of different colours.

In his last major novel, Dickens explores the nature of hybridity: racial, cultural, sexual. As in so much of the Sensation fiction of the 1860s, the real mystery that needs to be solved is not the identity of whoever is responsible for the victim's death, but the responsibility of identity. Dickens had already recognized the complexity of questions about the construction of the self, emphasizing the pressures of ideology and forms of discipline, but, if his previous work included detailed diagnostic treatments of characters organized around their passions, none of his earlier writing was so thoroughly engrossed by the contradictory workings of desire. With *Edwin Drood* he was redeploying some familiar situations and familiar sets of images, but introducing new kinds of motivation and changing the proportions of his design; the tonalities of 'Dr Marigold' and of his last book could not be more different; there is no mistaking the seriousness of Dickens's intentions in the final phase of his working life. He was extending the territory of the imagination inwards. In the end, he finished less than half of the projected number of instalments: more than enough to see the slant it gives to his career, concluding with a new beginning.

Notes

CHAPTER 1. STREETWISE

1. Edgar Allan Poe, *The Fall of the House of Usher, and Other Writings*, ed. David Galloway (Harmondsworth: Penguin Books, 1986), 188.

CHAPTER 2. THE IMAGE OF THE CHILD

1. See J. C. Drummond and Anne Wilbraham, *The Englishman's Food* (London: Pimlico, 1991), 364.

CHAPTER 5. TAKING THE ROOF OFF

1. John Ruskin, 'Fiction, Fair or Foul', *Nineteenth Century*, 7 (June 1880), 945.

CHAPTER 6. THE STUPENDOUS POWER OF MONEY

1. John Forster, *The Life of Charles Dickens*, i (London: Chapman & Hall, 1872), 48.
2. Ibid.
3. Ibid.

Select Bibliography

WORKS BY CHARLES DICKENS

The Clarendon Dickens (Oxford: Clarendon Press, 1966 (in progress)). The most authoritative edition of Dickens's novels. The standard scholarly edition, collating manuscripts and editions published in Dickens's lifetime, but lacking annotation. The Clarendon texts are being used in the World's Classics series (Oxford: Oxford University Press), which adds annotation.

Of other paperback editions available, those in the Penguin English Library series include the most reliable combinations of text, critical introduction, and commentary, and have been used in the preparation of this book.

Dickens's Working Notes for his Novels, ed. Harry Stone (Chicago: University of Chicago Press, 1987).

The Dent Uniform Edition of Dickens's Journalism, ed. Michael Slater (London: J. M. Dent, 1994–2000). Four volumes: Volume One, 1833–39, includes *Sketches by Boz;* Volume Two, 1834–51, consists of a variety of reports, essays, and reviews; Volume Three, 1851–59, includes sixty-five articles from *Household Words;* Volume Four, 1859–70, includes *The Uncommercial Traveller* and a few other pieces.

The Pilgrim Edition of the Letters of Charles Dickens, ed. Madeline House, Graham Storey, Kathleen Tillotson, *et al.* (Oxford: Clarendon Press, 1965 (in progress)). Eleven volumes so far, covering the period 1820–67.

Charles Dickens: The Public Readings, ed. Philip Collins (Oxford Clarendon Press, 1975).

The Speeches of Charles Dickens, ed. K. J. Fielding (Oxford: Clarendon Press, 1960).

BIBLIOGRAPHY

Chittick, Kathryn, *The Critical Reception of Charles Dickens, 1833–1841* (New York: Garland, 1989).

Cohn, Alan M., and Collins, K. K, *The Cumulated Dickens Checklist 1970–79* (Troy, NY: Whitston Publishing Company, 1982).

Fenstermaker, John J., *Charles Dickens, 1940–1975: An Analytical Subject Index to Periodical Criticism of the Novels and Christmas Books* (London: George Prior, 1979).

Gold, Joseph, *The Stature of Dickens: A Centenary Bibliography of Dickensian Criticism 1836–1975* (London: Macmillan, 1975).

PERIODICALS

The Dickensian. Journal of the Dickens Fellowship. London, 1905–.

Dickens Studies. Boston: Emerson College, 1965–9. Continued as *Dickens Studies Annual* (Carbondale, Ill.: Southern Illinois University Press, 1970).

Dickens Studies Newsletter. Louisville, Ky., 1970–83. Continued as *Dickens Quarterly* (Louisville, Ky., 1984). Published by the Dickens Society. Publishes regular bibliographies of Dickens criticism.

BIOGRAPHY

Ackroyd, Peter, *Dickens* (London: Sinclair-Stevenson, 1990). The most enjoyable biography, in some respects the most Dickensian in terms of its imaginative energy.

Allen, Michael, *Charles Dickens's Childhood* (Basingstoke: Macmillan, 1988).

Butt, John, and Tillotson, Kathleen, *Dickens at Work* (London: Methuen, 1957).

Forster, John, *The Life of Charles Dickens*, 3 vols. (London: Chapman & Hall, 1872–4). The earliest comprehensive account of Dickens's life, and still invaluable. Written by Dickens's son-in-law; contains the notorious 'Autobiographical Fragment'.

Johnson, Edgar, *Charles Dickens: His Tragedy and Triumph* (New York: Simon & Schuster, 1952). Still the standard modern biography.

Kaplan, Fred, *Dickens: A Biography* (London: Hodder & Stoughton, 1988). Concentrates on the autobiographical basis and significance of several of the major texts.

Slater, Michael, *Dickens and Women* (London: André Deutsch, 1983).

Tomalin, Claire, *The Invisible Woman: The Story of Nelly Ternan and Charles Dickens* (London: Penguin Books, 1991). Feminist biographical account of the relationship between Dickens and the actress who became his mistress.

CRITICISM

NOTE: There is a huge volume of critical writing on Dickens. The following list of titles is a selection of those books that include discussions judged to be particularly insightful or influential.

Andrews, Malcolm, *Dickens and the Grown-Up Child* (London: Macmillan, 1994).

Brooks, Peter, *Reading for the Plot: Design and Intention in Narrative* (Oxford: Oxford University Press, 1984). Includes an important essay on *Great Expectations* that views the construction of narrative in terms of a powerful psychological dynamic suggested by Freud's *Beyond the Pleasure Principle.*

Carey, John, *The Violent Effigy: A Study of Dickens's Imagination* (London: Faber & Faber, 1973). A highly personal reading of the novels that includes a number of useful individual insights delivered with a characteristically vivid turn of phrase.

Collins, Philip, *Dickens and Crime* (London: Macmillan, 1962). This and the following title act as the most useful introductory guides to their given topics.

—— *Dickens and Education* (London: Macmillan, 1964).

Connor, Steven, *Charles Dickens* (Oxford: Basil Blackwell, 1985). A useful compendium of recent theoretical approaches to Dickens (post-structuralist, deconstructive, Lacanian).

—— (ed.), *Charles Dickens: A Critical Reader* (London: Longman, 1996).

Gallagher, Catherine, *The Industrial Reformation of English Fiction, 1832–1867* (Chicago: Chicago University Press, 1985). Concerned with the relationship between literary form and social historical constraints.

Gilmour, Robin, *The Idea of the Gentleman in Victorian Fiction* (London: Allen & Unwin, 1981). Places Dickens in the context of Victorian social norms and codes of behaviour.

Ingham, Patricia, *Dickens, Women and Language* (London: Harvester Wheatsheaf, 1992). Highly compact and suggestive exploration of gender issues.

Kucich, John, *Repression in Victorian Fiction: Charlotte Brontë, George Eliot and Charles Dickens* (Berkeley and Los Angeles: University of California Press, 1987). Focuses on the historical construction of Victorian subjectivity with particular reference to the encrypting of

sexual identity.
Leavis, F. R, and Leavis, Q. D, *Dickens the Novelist* (London: Chatto & Windus, 1970). A landmark in traditional criticism of Dickens, despite being strongly opinionated about the rank order of the novels in terms of artistic integrity.
McKnight, Natalie, *Idiots, Madmen and Other Prisoners in Dickens* (London: Macmillan, 1993).
Miller, D. A., *The Novel and the Police* (Berkeley and Los Angeles: University of California Press, 1988). A dazzling analysis of the ways in which Victorian fiction is complicit with a variety of forms of social discipline.
Miller, J. Hillis, *Charles Dickens: The World of his Novels* (Cambridge, Mass.: Harvard University Press, 1958). A phenomenological account that provides an extraordinarily comprehensive and systematic interpretation of the ruling motifs in the novels.
Monod, Sylvere, *Dickens the Novelist* (Norman, Okla.: University of Oklahoma Press, 1968). A very full treatment along traditional lines of the thematic emphases of the major novels.
Moretti, Franco, *The Way of the World: The Bildungsroman and European Culture* (London: Verso, 1987). Unignorable survey of the nineteenth-century novel of personal development; includes some extremely stimulating, and provocative, discussions of Dickens.
Morris, Pam, *Dickens's Class Consciousness* (London: Macmillan, 1991).
Musselwhite, David, *Partings Welded Together: Politics and Desire in the Nineteenth Century Novel* (London: Methuen, 1988). Unusually, concentrates on Dickens's very earliest work, arguing for the exceptional brilliance of *Sketches by Boz.*
Poovey, Mary, *Uneven Developments: the Ideological Work of Gender in Mid-Victorian England* (Chicago: Chicago University Press, 1988). Focuses on the relationship between text, context and reader in respect of narratives of individual development.
Sadrin, Anny, *Parentage and Inheritance in the Novels of Charles Dickens* (Cambridge: Cambridge University Press, 1994)
Schad, S. J, *The Reader in the Dickensian Mirrors: Some New Language* (London: Macmillan, 1992)
Schlicke, Paul, *Dickens and Popular Entertainment* (London: Allen & Unwin, 1984).
Sedgwick, Eve Kosofsky, *Between Men: English Literature and Male Homosocial Desire* (New York: Columbia University Press, 1985). Examines the relationship between homosocial bonding and other forms of social relationship and patterns of desire in nineteenth-century writing.
Stewart, Garrett, *Dickens and the Trials of the Imagination* (Cambridge, Mass.: Harvard University Press, 1974).

Tambling, Jeremy, *Dickens, Violence and Modern State: Dreams of the Scaffold* (London: Macmillan, 1995). Explores Dickens's interest in forms of discipline from a Foucauldian perspective.

Trotter, David, *Circulation: Defoe, Dickens and the Economies of the Novel* (London: Macmillan, 1988). Brilliant exploration of how the circulation of blood is used as a metaphor for various kinds of urban development in literary and other texts.

Welsh, Alexander, *The City of Dickens* (Oxford: Clarendon Press, 1971). Makes good use of Dickens's journalism.

—— *From Copyright to Copperfield: The Identity of Dickens* (Cambridge, Mass.: Harvard University Press, 1987). Particularly good at using biographical data in relating Dickens's own sense of self to contemporaneous models of subjectivity.

Westburg, Barry, *The Confessional Fictions of Charles Dickens* (De Kalb, Ill.: Northern Illinois University Press, 1977). A thoroughgoing Lacanian analysis of Dickens's writing in the first person.

Index

American English 44, 48
Argus (Panoptes) 42, 74, 94
Australia (as destination) 67, 70

Bentham, Jeremy 42, 94
Blind, Asylum for the, 43
Boston, Mass. 43, 46
Bridgeman, Laura 44, 47, 122
British Association for the Advancement of Science 5
British Museum 75
Burton's Gentleman's Magazine 3

Carlyle, Thomas 77
Caswell, Oliver 122
Census of 1851 1
Charles I 57–8, 59, 62
Cholera 78
Collins, Wilkie 85
Cornhill (associated with Mayday rioting) 37
Coutts, Angela Burdett 68
Cyclopean eye 74, 76

Detectives 72–6
Dickens, Charles:
  All the Year Round 85
  American Notes for General Circulation 41–8, 122
  'Autobiographical fragment' 89
  Barnaby Rudge 30, 37–41, 42
  Bleak House 72–83
  Child's History of England, A 57
  David Copperfield 52–71, 76, 81
  'Detective Police' 72, 76
  'Dr Marigold's Prescriptions' 120–3
  Dombey and Son 34–6
  Edwin Drood 123–6
  Great Expectations 76, 84–101
  Hard Times 50–1
  Household Words 72, 75
  Little Dorrit 82–3
  Martin Chuzzlewit 48–50
  Mudfog Association 5
  Nicholas Nickleby 27–30
  Old Curiosity Shop 30–4
  Oliver Twist 21–7
  'On Duty with Inspector Field' 72–5
  Our Mutual Friend 102–6, 108–119
  The Pickwick Papers 5–20, 54, 67, 100
  Sketches by Boz 1–5

A Tale of Two Cities 30, 47, 84–5
Dickens, John (father); his imprisonment for debt 18, 20
Diet (working class) 21–2, 30

Eastern Penitentiary (Pennsylvania) 46
Education 21
Emigration 69–70, 123

Fallen women 66–70
Forster, John 56, 89
Foxe's *Book of Martyrs* 61

Gordon Riots (1780) 37
Great Exhibition 74–5, 78

Intramural interment 78

Lever, Charles 85
Lancet, The 21
Lazarus, story of 63
Liberty (in America) 45–7

Marshalsea prison 82

Phrenology 3–4, 49
Poe, Edgar Allen 3–4, 38
Poor Law (1834) 27
Poor Law Commissioners 21

Reform Bill (1832) 20
Ruskin, John 78

Serial publication 65, 84–5, 87, 88–9, 101
Society for the Diffusion of Useful Knowledge 5
Shakespeare:
Hamlet 63
Macbeth 63
Spitting 45

Urania Cottage 68–9, 123
Warren's Blacking 89
Washington, DC 45
Worcester, Mass. 43
Wordsworth 24–5, 82